The Accident Stager

SUSAN MOSS

COVER PAINTING: Flame Pond

Flame Pond (for Japan) oil on canvas, 6 ft. x 4 ft. 2011 Susan Moss, FRONTISPIECE:
Black Peace Pond, oil on canvas 60 in. x 54 in. 2010 Susan Moss, AUTHOR PHOTO:
Intersection, oil on canvas 32 in. x 60 in. 2010 Susan Moss.

Re: Source Publications

4767 York Blvd.

Los Angeles, California 90042

ISBN: 0964232944

ISBN 13: 9780964232945

To Amy Hecht Moss, 1920-2011 for her unswerving faith and encouragement, her generosity and kindness, her love and wisdom, for sixty-seven years of my life.

Chapter One

Gaude Velasquez (called Gus) admired his lean, tall, model-perfect figure in the slightly peeling mirror of the Suits R Us clothing store. He had slipped on their Sale of the Week item, a polyester-rayon suit that, though of thin and slightly sleazy material with an unnatural shine, suited him. A suit that suited him at Suits R Us, Gus thought with a chuckle. It would do nicely for his professional presentation.

He was acutely aware that his last name was the same as the great Spanish painter who had painted his figurative canvases in the Royal Palace: the King, the Queen, their child and assorted amusing people like the ugly midget that entertained the royalty with his sleight-of-hand magic tricks. Gus had seen a reproduction of a painting Diego Velasquez had done, a self-portrait of the artist, brushing paint on his canvas while surrounded by his amusing milieu.

Gus's chosen profession also required a certain artistry and skill, timing, persistence and a sort of gutsy courage and daring, not found in many other lines of work. He prided himself in his

1

work as a con artist of immense talent. He had mastered this skill and it had paid off despite the risks he took. And it *was* risky. Someone could, theoretically, get killed. He had to pull off the "accident" so it looked like he had the "right of way." It was a bit of a magic act, taking a good shot of adrenaline and causing his heart to hammer in his chest. But if done accurately, it was: *fool the eye, fool the insurance company, fool the victim.* Fool everyone except himself. "Ha, ha," he laughed in the empty changing room, hearing his voice reverberate. Gus exited the room giddy with triumph, smoothing his slicked brown hair with his graceful, long fingers.

"I'll take it," he told the salesperson, a meek young fellow with blemished facial skin. Gus had gotten out of the new pants and jacket, put on his khakis and plaid shirt, his thin socks and worn loafers, and gone on to the cash register. He had just received a check from Mainstay Insurance Company, a reliable payer. He might just buy his wife, Maria, a little jewelry, perhaps an imitation diamond ring. Zircon looked better than glass and was just a little more expensive. She would love it. Maria deserved something special, after all the auto insurance he carried was under her name. Any insurance company checking out her record would see it was perfectly clean.

The kids might get something too, a little reward. He had three children now; Jorge was nine, Juanita was almost eight, and Juan was only sixteen months. He would look around the mall for something. Juanita loved picture books and Juan would be content with a stuffed toy or maybe a toy car. Jorge was too old for toys. Gus would get him a book at the Barnes and Noble.

Velasquez suddenly had the idea of incorporating the children into his work, realizing that they would up the ante. He would make more money with them riding in the car with him. He would be very careful so they did not get hurt too much. Soft tissue injury, sprains and strains, back and neck injuries, the children could easily surmount in less than a month. Of course there would be some vertigo. He himself had suffered from it, feeling dizzy throughout the day following a crash. But prize-fighters suffered injuries too. If done cleanly, there was no bloody mess to horrify anyone. These were internal injuries, hardly even noticeable. No one would even comment. And the pain and dizziness never lasted more than a month or so.

Meanwhile this was an easy way to make money. He had become very successful at it—small-time crime. No one ever suspected him. He had never killed anyone, after all. Others might rob banks or murder some innocent victim in an attempt to divest the poor slob of his money. This type of crime simply wasn't for Gaude Velasquez. For one thing, it was too simple of a crime and too easy to get caught. He reveled in complex situations, like a magician, all smoke and mirrors, manipulating his victim, hypnotizing them to feel guilty. Split-second timing was his forte. Prison held zero interest for him.

Accident-staging was simple, fast, clean work. If you were quick and clever with good timing, accident staging was a lucrative profession. He prided himself on his smooth approach. He just needed the name, insurance information, registration, license number and address of the victim. He handled all this information gathering efficiently, with a satin-smooth tone of voice. He was even able to persuade the victim to take the blame! Ha!

He could talk a fat lady out of her Haagen-Dazs.

Velasquez took his suit, wrapped in plastic sheathing, and laid it carefully over his arm. He then turned on his heels, pirouetting like a dancer, and headed for other parts of the mall to find gifts for his family.

"Hello Shortie!" Gus was surprised, as he walked down the long corridor in the mall, to see a partner in crime, a former "intern." He recalled when two of his cohorts had pulled a "Swoop and Squat" in front of a teenager who had probably only just passed Drivers Training. That involved Manuel Diaz also, with the three of them coordinating their efforts. When Shortie had suddenly swooped in front of the unsuspecting young driver, then hit the brakes, Manuel had, from behind, crashed into the novice. Gus, behind Manuel had dented Manuel's bumper in front of him, also injuring his own car. The police came and decided that the teenager, Ben, had been at fault for not driving defensively, following too closely, negligence, etc. and Manuel had collected the money from the insurance company, divvying it up between the three of them.

The poor teenager, Gus remembered, had been terrorized, left stuttering and shaking and he had profusely apologized. A tape-recorder hidden in Gus's vest pocket had picked up the "confession." That was always the pleasure in this type of work, seeing the victim shaking and quaking. It satisfied an unconscious sadistic streak. He loved to watch the victim admit guilt, say they were sorry, grovel before him, and then get blamed for the "accident." The black mark would go on *their* driving record, while he himself remained clean as a freshly laundered T-shirt. They would get a hefty insurance rate-hike, while he collected a fat payment.

"How goes it, Shortie?" Gus was in a good mood. He was sometimes temperamental and, once in a while, violently angry. People had remarked that Velasquez could be cruel. Well, they really had no idea how cruel, did they?

"Oh, really well, Gus. I just got a check from Everystate Insurance. I took my boy, Carlos with me in the car and he got a little head and neck pain. He's twelve now. I wouldn't take him when he was younger. Developing kids are too vulnerable. He got me a nice check. He'll be fine in a month. He's very strong. He didn't even scream."

"You're really good at it. It's all in the timing and you're now a crackerjack. Who did you hit?"

"Oh, just an old lady who couldn't see too well. Of course they blamed her for backing out of her driveway. I didn't hit her too hard. Just enough, you know. Spun her around like a carousel."

"Good work!"

"How about you? I see you've shopped."

"Yep! Mainstay Insurance, always reliable," Gus laughed. "Got a fellow by a wicked sideswipe after he turned right. Told him he should have looked!" Velasquez was feeling confident, perhaps overconfident. It was always good to get a job over and done with. He did feel a little dizzy but that would pass. Shortie looked just a tad out of focus. Gus squinted his eyes.

"How about a beer across the street?" Gus suggested. A drink might just be what he needed right now. There was a little bar called Jazz next to the Italian bakery. A cold German beer would help him stabilize.

"Sure, got some time. Only work part-time now!" Shortie laughed.

Shortie was a small, squat man, well-built with bulging muscles. His black hair had turned gray. At one time he had been a mason and a brick-layer. But times were tough now, he had been laid off. Still he had skills and a degree of artistry most people never developed. At work they had called him "Shortie," though his real name was Tomas. He had enjoyed doing honest work, even though it was hard labor. He had sweated long hours under the hot Los Angeles sun in the summer, the season many of the jobs came in, from sunrise to sunset. But then construction work dried up.

This accident work, though illegal and dangerous, was quick. One job took care of his family for several months and he had plenty of time to spend with them. Once an honest man, Tomas had turned to petty crime. And it paid well he soon discovered, even better than honest sweat. As long as they didn't get caught… He made sure there were no police or Highway Patrol around when he exploited a situation that could easily have been a "right of way" accident.

"How're Juanita, Juan and Jorge?"

"They're great! Juanita is very smart. I'm thinking she would be a good side-kick. I found a junk Mercedes, 1982, with a few scratches for a thousand dollars at the swap meet. It's white. Or at least it was once before the dust settled," he laughed " Perfect for the next job."

"Is Juan walking yet?"

"Oh, yes, he toddles around. I don't know what he's thinking. But he likes to go riding around the city. We pick a neighborhood and scout it out. Sometimes Jorge comes with us, but he's a bookworm and likes to stay home and read now."

"So what's on the horizon?" Shortie asked.

"We live on the street parallel to a run-down neighborhood where artists have studios. There's a small post-office with a narrow driveway. So dangerous. You really can't see much coming out of it, especially if a big car or truck is parked at the mailboxes, blocking the view. They just changed the street to only two lanes. Just perfect. Ha! The City made it perfect for accidents! They probably changed it so people could get out of their parked cars safely. Little did the City know what they also did! Think we'll give that one a try next."

The two men quickly walked across the street to the bar, being especially careful to look both ways.

Chapter Two

Joy Bravitski opened the heavy garage door to her sky-lit studio. "This door weighs a ton," she muttered to herself as she groaned and heaved. This exercise ritual happened each weekday morning without fail. She was a disciplined artist who did not depend upon "inspiration" to paint and draw but showed up at the studio around nine, or shortly thereafter, Monday through Friday and sometimes Saturday also, to go to work. Even though she was now retirement age, sixty-six in fact, a whole year past retirement age, Joy worked as regularly as when she had been thirty-three. The heavy garage door seemed to get heavier every time she opened it. Joy reminded herself that it kept her in shape.

She owed her remarkably youthful appearance to her creative life. People guessed her age to be forty or fifty, at most. Joy had a slender body of medium height which she kept flexible through swimming laps, and strong through weight-lifting and exercise machines, besides the garage door. She was rarely ill.

Joy brushed her dark hair aside. Hair dye was a necessity now. Other than that, she barely wore makeup: a touch of eye-liner, violet-smoke Channel, her one extravagance to line her steady brown eyes. Joy rationalized that the pencil lasted half a year. She got inexpensive lipstick from the drugstore and her rouge was from a free sample she had been given.

She wore old, painted-up clothes. Joy joked that the holes in her jeans were authentic. She was fashionable! Her woven cotton tops and turtlenecks had seen too many laundry days and were faded, shapeless, sad articles. Wearing new clothes to the studio was always a mistake, as paint had a way of smearing up and onto everything in sight. She had ruined too many new outfits with unplanned splashes and drips.

The back door had a steel bar across the front of it. Once some boys had tried to break in and installing a metal tube running across the door, caught at the sides by two steel rings, had acted as a bolt. Joy tugged it open. The open door revealed the neighborhood skunk, sound asleep in the stairwell.

"Go!" Joy ordered the sleepy creature that obligingly, if resentfully, slowly got up and quietly, without squirting its sickening, odorous defense, sauntered off into the backyard. This skunk was tame and obedient. No burned rubber-stink to perfume the studio today. "Thanks, Skunky," she cheerfully called as the little wild animal waddled away.

Joy watered her plants and planned her day. The empty canvas on her painting board was of medium size. She liked best to work very large: six, seven, eight foot canvases suited her best. But she had to make sales to keep her studio as well as the new Silverado Chevy truck she had put a down-payment on, now parked proudly in front of her studio. Its ownership required monthly payments, an obligation that created a need. Medium and smaller work were sometimes easier to sell.

She had worried about money her whole life. Her art was good enough to sell, to show at galleries and museums. People loved it. Yet the economy was depressed and it seemed her career had run out of gas. Still, Joy sputtered along, working with the same diligence with which she had worked when the big trucks had pulled up with two guys jumping out to load the paintings. The truck would then drive off to her next gallery or museum show where Bravitski would appear at the opening. Soon Joy would find checks in her mail from the gallery's various collectors. But no one seemed to care if she appeared now. In fact, they probably would like her to disappear.

All the show and sales activity had abruptly ended some time ago. How long? She couldn't recall and even if she could, it was all too depressing. The past was a haze: meanwhile the paintings had piled up in stacks and the paper-drawers were full of unsold drawings, a cruel reminder each morning that her career had been sinking for way too long. Her ship had, in fact, sunk.

She brushed away cobwebs of doubt and paralyzing fear, took out a long sheet of freezer wrap she used as a palette, and began to squeeze out the expensive, but exquisite oil colors which squiggled out of the tube like happy snakes at a picnic. How exciting the colors were! Joy couldn't wait to dip a brush into them and apply the loaded implement to the heavy, sized paper she was using for a study. The necessity to apply them with hope and optimism was a given, even though she had only just thrown away a study that had bleakly turned into mud. This one would work. It just had to.

With the landscape of California in mind, Joy sank her brush into a green, then a blue, mixing them as they went onto the paper as a permutation of liquid sky. Although the abstracts she invented were void of figurative elements, the environment was never far from her subconscious. Joy loved to drive through the lush, inspiring countryside on sojourns to San Francisco, for instance, where she had shown her work for thirty years at the San Francisco Museum of Modern Art Artist's Gallery. The Director, always enthusiastic about her Art, had retired. The new Director of the gallery, located in Fort Mason, wanted only Bay Area artists, excluding Joy who lived in Los Angeles.

The new Director had tried to dismiss her, but Joy's work kept renting and selling. She had managed to hang in there another year. But then what? They refused to take more work even though it easily rented and sold. Only two drawings were left, both rented out.

Joy badly needed new outlets, new galleries for her work. Lately, she had gotten a cover for her truck-bed so she could bring art to show galleries. Photographs and CDs just weren't as good. Bringing the actual paintings worked out much better. They could take one on consignment, meaning that they would try to sell it and pay her only if they succeeded. This sometimes took months or years. Or dismally, they would return it.

Joy had installed a lock on her truck bed cover so she could stop for lunch without worrying about abandoning the vehicle for an hour. Her truck was an important part of her little business, even as scant as sales had been lately.

She reached for a brilliant yellow, stroking it across the page, a blaze of sunlight. As Joy worked she listened to a classical radio station. Vivaldi's "Summer" from his *Four Seasons* was being played, the perfect accompaniment. She also loved Beethoven, Bach and Rachmaninoff. At one time she had played rock music while working but her taste had changed over the years. Now the background music had to be classical symphonies, piano concertos, and etudes by the great composers. Joy had an infectious smile that now came onto her face as she thought of the orchestrations she loved. The music always brought a flood of memories. Beethoven brought back memories of an old boyfriend who told her she painted like he composed.

Times were tough but music was a great solace and stimulus to her creativity.

Yes, there had been much better times and it was with fortitude and longing that she imagined that they would return. She knew she would have her "comeback" but when would it ever happen? She hoped she was still alive and well when the Art World would finally gave her recognition.

In her mind's eye, Joy saw her show on Madison Avenue in New York City when she had been only thirty-two years old. She had landed at the top of the heap, not because of years of experience, but because of some strong paintings plus a large, heaping dose of beginner's luck. No pounding of the sidewalks or years of entry fees into juried shows had been necessary.

Getting out of the yellow cab on tony Madison Avenue in uptown New York City, she had stepped toward the David Fine Gallery. "What a glorious place to have my first solo show in New York," she thought. Joy was excited and honored. It was a sunny but cool March day and the city had glittered and gleamed. She felt a part of the cosmopolitan city, so rich in culture and sophistication. She was a New Yorker for a day.

It had all happened as if by a witch with a magic wand. A smart, aggressive agent she had been working with had somehow arranged this incredible opportunity.

Immediately in front of her in the large plate-glass window was *Swarm*, a seven-by-five foot layered painting in transparent mauves, cocoas and purples. It had been borrowed back as it was already sold to a young collector, Martha Mull, who had ridden past the gallery on her bicycle.

"I want to buy that painting," she had told David Fine.

"Do you have a place big enough?" he asked her.

"If we don't, we'll move."

This courageous lady, so sure of her taste, would someday own two galleries in New York. She would sell many more works for Joy, even before she became an art dealer in her own right.

Martha, an energetic and sophisticated young lady, would invite Joy to gourmet dinners she prepared herself. She admired Martha' skills and intelligence. She had seen something in Joy's painting, and even though it did not come with a major reputation, had bought it. She had trusted her own judgment. This was a rarity in the art world.

The added benefit of having collectors was that they often became friends. Martha would become one, a benefit that enriched both their lives. Joy loved New York but only for a short visit. She would get a shot in the arm of energy and excitement before returning to the quiet of her California life where she could create in peace.

David Fine continued to sell her paintings and drawings. She would receive the checks in the mail and then walk down the street to the bank. It all seemed so easy. Just paint in L.A., ship the work to New York, have a terrific opening, fly home, wait for the mailman, go to the bank. Other galleries and museums in other cities and states followed. More checks flowed in. Joy had been able to do what she loved, what she was born to accomplish, even if it was at times hard, messy work. The encouragement and support she received was almost magical as someone came through with a check most of the time, whenever she was in need. She could chide herself on needless worrying.

But that was then. This was now. Joy muttered encouragement to herself, the only encouragement she received now, as she picked up another brush to mix a purplish-blue.

Now she seemed to reside in Rejection City. Whereas once she didn't even have to apply, now her slides and CDs came back with a short note beginning with the word, "Unfortunately…" Galleries were "full" and juried shows were inundated with so much other strong work. "We're sorry, but unfortunately we have to inform you that your work will not be included in our…"

She did succeed in one juried show and even got an Honorable Mention, a piece of paper congratulating her. But her drawing had not sold. She decided not to enter any more juried shows. They were for beginners. She was wasting her time. She would just have to wait for the opportunities that would elevate her to the level she had once obtained so easily. Or higher! Something or someone would lead to her "rediscovery."

Joy felt irritated and frustrated by the void that had once been filled with shows and sales. Always worrying about the bills wore her down. Yet she had a die-hard faith in her work that never wavered. Even when the phone stopped ringing with opportunities, she never gave up hope. She knew her work was strong.

"Most artists go through this," Joy reassured herself. Even Rembrandt had gone "out of style" and at the end of his life had gone bankrupt, having to sell all his possessions including his home and studio props from which he concocted his masterpieces. Hard to imagine how the rejection of one of the greatest artists in the whole history of art had happened. Yet his brown glazes had gone out of style when high-tone jeweled colors became the fashion. No one had wanted Rembrandts! His son, Titus, had tried but failed to help him sell his work. Today any Rembrandt painting would fetch millions. However, most, if not all, were in museums and would never even come up at auction. If only Rembrandt could look down from Heaven or wherever his soul went, and see how revered and valuable his paintings and etchings had become!

But, somehow, this recollection, this comparison, did not help Joy with her slight depression, though she never sank too far down. Her creative work did not allow it. There was so much joy in Joy, she always rose back up. "What do they know?" she decided and kept working.

Her studio day, with a break for lunch, went quickly because she loved her work. Joy remembered the time at the gym in the locker room when she had loudly proclaimed, "I can't wait to go to work!" Every startled head had turned. Most people disliked their jobs. Some hated them. She felt very fortunate, indeed.

Joy finished her study and her day came to an end. Cleaning her brushes, she prepared to go home to feed her cat, Brandy. Joy had gotten Brandy as a kitten at the Lacy Street Pound when some rats had invaded her little house. Brandy, still a tiny kitten, had confronted those tiny thieves who would steal into the kitchen after Joy went to bed. With a stiff growl, surprising in such a tiny baby cat, Brandy had marched into the kitchen and told those rats in no uncertain terms where to go! They had squealed in shocked surprise, "slammed" the pantry door shut, and run for their lives. They had learned their lesson and not returned. Joy had heard this all as she lay in bed and chuckled.

The next morning Brandy sat in the kitchen and smiled.

Joy would make some phone calls at home. She made calls to collectors to try to sell her work, to galleries to try to entice them over to her studio. But once a day she allowed herself a personal call. Her friend, Carey, had a similar career, writing screenplays by herself. So these two had meshed, needing a little conversation every day to break up the loneliness inherent in their creative lives.

She hadn't spoken to Carey today, so she would call her after she had fed Brandy who ate chopped carrots along with her dry kitty-food and treats. Joy knew the carrots would help Brandy's eyesight, as well as help prevent Cancer. Animals also got that terrible disease.

And Brandy loved her carrots, refusing to eat her dry food unless the chopped, crunchy orange pieces were mixed in.

"Brandy, you are such a smart cat!" Joy petted the cat's silky coat as she ate her mixed fresh and dried food. "You're so beautiful too." Brandy was mostly black-and-white with a Lone-Ranger's mask on her white face and a saddle-blanket of black and brown on her white body. She had black leggings above white paws and a black tail with a white tip. Her wide green eyes were utterly expressive. Brandy's strong personality and flirtatious attitude captivated everyone in the neighborhood. She was also a natural comedian, getting up on the roof and stretching her neck to look at Joy through the window, her face upside-down.

After feeding Brandy, Joy picked up the phone and dialed Carey's number. "What's happening?" Joy asked when her friend picked up.

"This screenplay is driving me up the wall. It's called *Mixed Messages* and that's exactly what I'm getting from it."

"Sounds exciting, though. What's it about?"

"Oh, a romance gone wrong. It's about communication or lack thereof."

"So that wrecks the relationship?'

"For sure. But I'm working on retrieving it."

"How does it get revived?"

"The couple has to learn how to effectively communicate with each other. It's a slow, agonizing process. How's your work going?"

"The study is done. I'm going to start the canvas tomorrow."

"I love your work. Your color sense is so acute. I've got those small pieces you had in your sale last year right by my desk. Very inspirational!"

"Thanks. Have you heard from your friend Stan?"

"Oh, Stan. You know he disappears for months at a time. He's a professional stand-up comedian, so he's on the road. Gives me time to work, however. I shouldn't complain."

"He's a good guy, though. You probably wouldn't want a man around full- time. You'd complain he was being a nuisance!"

"You're right. He's great in small doses. He keeps me doubled over with laughter. He cheers me up. Life is too depressing without him."

"I gave up men long ago. Just didn't seem to have the craving anymore. You know I always had a Saturday night date without fail. I thought I would die if a man wasn't calling me! Now a movie with you is my favorite evening." Joy enthused.

"Thanks. Maybe we can see something when you come back from Reno."

"Yes, we're celebrating my Mom's ninetieth birthday!"

"That's fabulous! What a wonderful long life. You must have inherited good genes. Have a wonderful trip! I'll talk to you before you go."

"Thanks. I hope my genes enable me to live through this recession! Talk to you soon."

Joy hung up and went to the kitchen to prepare her simple dinner. Tonight it would be stir-fried vegetables over rice with almonds, dill, cilantro and soy sauce. She wasn't a total vegetarian, but at least two or three dinners a week excluded meat. A total health-nut might be more conscientious, but she did enough healthy things to stay well.

For instance, the "Y" was an integral part of her life. Three times a week she rose before 5 a.m. to work out with machines, weights, and sit-up slant-boards, followed by a forty-five minute swim in the Olympic-size pool. This routine kept her energetic, healthy and enthusiastic about her life. Aches and pains would soon vanish.

Although Jewish, Joy had taken up Buddhism and chanted to her Gohonzon, a scroll with calligraphy in Sanskrit, before going to bed. Tonight she visualized her career being revived as she chanted the Lotus Sutra. Something would have to happen soon. She just couldn't sustain her painting without support.

After chanting, she got into her pajamas. Brandy hopped onto the bed.

"Do you want to be brushed?" she asked Brandy. The cat purred.

Joy took the natural bristle brush and gave Brandy strokes from head to tail while the cat licked her other hand. It had been a surprise when Brandy loved being brushed as the cat hardly let anyone do anything to her. She would paw anyone off, striking them with her claws. Even the Vet had to use anesthesia to stitch up Brandy's wounds once when she got into a cat fight. When Joy had bought the brush, she wondered if Brandy would ever let her use it. But now, Brandy, content, was dropping off to sleep. Joy joined her shortly and was soon dreaming of her colors,

Chapter Three

Joy rose early. At a quarter to five, she let Brandy go outside for a while. She then picked out clean work clothes from her closet, got her Y canvas-tote out filled with her work-out clothes and swimming suit, and prepared to greet the day. She believed in the "early to bed, early to rise" axiom. Whether it would make her healthy, wealthy and wise was another story, however. She felt rested and energetic. Joy would do her machines, her swim and then, after a smoothie, go to the studio to begin the new canvas. This made her excited enough to get up.

At the gym she did her sit-ups on the slant board, her leg-raises on the Roman Chair, the pull and push for her arms on the various machines. An *Art in America* magazine would keep her mind occupied while she pushed her legs against a weighted platform. She then slipped on her bathing suit for her forty-five minute swim.

"The water is good today," Ronnie, a diminutive attorney with two children, remarked.

"Glad it is. How are your children?"

"We're going on holiday to Mexico next week. They're all excited."

"Have a great time. Where in Mexico are you going?"

"Puerto Vallarta and Yelapa."

"Oh, I went there on vacation with my sculptor friend, Gina. It's paradise. You'll love it." Yelapa had inspired many of Joy's paintings and drawings. *Voyage South,* a large six-foot oil had already gone through two collectors and was situated in a beautiful three-story townhouse by the ocean in Playa Del Ray. She had met the collector and would visit it occasionally.

"Yes, we're really looking forward to it." Ronnie smiled.

"See you when you come back." Joy smiled at Ronnie then headed for the pool.

How she loved to swim! The feather-light water enveloped her, carrying her along like a leaf in a stream. In the warmed water, she felt peaceful and refreshed. Her aches and pains from old injuries slowly vanished. Mostly she did the breast and side-strokes, as the water had too many chemicals to put her head under. She had been a lifeguard as a teenager and was good in emergencies. Before that, as a child, she had been skinny and weak, frightened of life, but her lifeguard job had given her a newfound strength.

Three-quarters of an hour later, Joy dried off and headed for the locker room. She showered and dressed in her work clothes, then blow-dried her hair. Joy then headed for her truck in the parking lot.

To Joy's consternation, there was a ticket on the windshield. What had she done wrong? She was perplexed. Once she had gotten a ticket in this very lot for not parking within the lines. But she had been extra careful since then. Her truck was parked correctly.

"No sticker?" she read, confused. Of course she had a registration sticker on the back saying 2011, a year ahead. This was still the summer of 2010. She was paid up. Then she noticed it said she did not have the month sticker. "How trivial is that?" she wondered. She did notice that her license plate had a place for a month sticker. But had they ever sent one from the DMV?

It seemed they invented new ways everyday to suck more cash out of her pocket.

A little annoyed, she drove home to make her smoothie and write a letter to the DMV. She wouldn't just pay this bill without an explanation. There was always some little annoyance or frustration to take care of, wasn't there? It seemed life was full of potholes one had to jump over.

Two weeks later, the DMV answered with the sticker. But she could not simply paste it on and forget it. She would have to show it to the Highway Patrol and have them sign it off. One more red-tape item to intrude upon her day.

Joy hated to interrupt her day. But the excuse came. A rude fellow habitually parked his tow truck in front of her studio.

"Jose's Tow. We Buy Cars 4 Cash," was the tacky sign on the back.

On this morning of July 13, an unlucky day, he not only let it idle, blasting the air in front of her studio with horrid fumes, he also let his back-up signal run so that every three seconds there was another annoying beep. Sometimes he let his truck idle for half-an-hour while he did his errands at the store down the street, talked on his cell phone, or adjusted his "catch," some wreck he had picked up for resale or scrap. She should call the Air Quality Management Board and complain. Her paintings, she was at pains to keep clean, were exposed to his dirty exhaust. She always felt totally frustrated by his carelessness. If she complained to him, he arrogantly screamed at her in some foreign language. Something about his right to park on the street.

Joy left the studio, closing the garage door. If he couldn't annoy her, maybe he would actually move his smelly truck! His macho attitude infuriated her.

The Highway Patrol was all the way downtown. But then she remembered downtown was only ten minutes away on the old Pasadena freeway. Joy didn't mind the drive. It calmed her down.

"Back your truck up," the Highway Patrol officer said to Joy after she found the building. He could see the sticker after she turned the truck around. He stamped the certificate and told her to send it in immediately.

Returning to the studio, Joy was delighted to see the tow truck gone. What a relief! She could work in peace.

She began the new canvas by laying it on the floor. She worked with brushes attached to long sticks of wood, swiping the color on with broad, sweeping strokes. When Joy was happy with what she had, she would put the canvas up against the wall. Sometimes the paint would drip, but she would incorporate this until it was drippy enough. Then she would lay the canvas back on the floor for more color. This process, back-and-forth, would go on the entire day. Painting was a mystery How it all coalesced into a painting was magical. Yet often it did.

Around four o'clock Joy cleaned her brushes. She would have to leave early today because she had to go to the post-office to mail her officially stamped sticker certificate and do some other errands. Usually she quit at five. But because her mother was turning ninety and there would be a celebration in Reno, Joy would be driving up with Chris. She would come back through San Francisco where there was an opening at the Artist's Gallery. Her two drawings were still rented out through August. She would also look for another gallery there.

Perhaps the gallery in Reno would take a work. Reno had one good gallery and a new Contemporary Art Museum. She would bring up several works. Also there was a gallery in Carmel that wanted to look, though he said he was "full." Still, he might like the work and think of someone who might buy it. It was worth a try.

Joy locked the studio door and headed for the post-office.

Chapter Four

Driving her new truck the short distance to the post-office up the street, Joy considered stopping by the mailboxes in front. But then the postal trucks liked to park there to load. She would block their path. Joy made the decision to go into the undersized parking lot.

One never knows where small decisions will lead. This thought popped into her head from nowhere. One had choices throughout the day. Which choice was right? Which choice would lead to dire consequences?

Joy entered the post-office and mailed in her sticker certificate. She then got back into her truck and headed for the driveway. As she reached the end of it, Joy saw a large truck was parked in front of the mailboxes to her right. She just couldn't see around it. The truck created a blind spot. But turning left was not an option. Even though she lived west of the post-office, turning right or east was the only safe way. She decided to wait it out until there was absolutely no one coming from the left. She had to get around that truck and that meant slow, cautious driving. She felt a bit paralyzed.

After a few minutes of waiting, the road cleared completely in both directions. Slowly, cautiously, Joy made her turn. She successfully made it around the truck and was heading for the light on Avenue 52, leaving behind the post office that was near Avenue 51. She breathed a sigh of relief.

Suddenly, she felt an energy pulling at her to her left. Glancing next to her she was shocked to see, going the wrong direction in the West-bound lane, a beat-up white Mercedes. The fellow driving was staring at her like a race-car driver intently sizing up his competition. He was thin and intense. What in the heck was going on? A shot of fear raced through her. Something was horribly wrong.

"What is this *weirdo* doing?' she muttered aloud. Her heart began racing. This strange guy was trouble; she had better get away from him right now. He was going the wrong way, in the wrong lane, and why was he staring at her? He gave her the creeps!

But just as she started to step on the gas to avoid him, he careened in front of her, catching her truck's bumper with the side of his car with a loud, horrible screech. He had fishtailed her; she had rear-ended him. The terrible sound reverberated in her brain. This sound meant only one thing. This sound meant damage. She immediately pulled over.

"Why didn't you slow down?" Joy asked indignantly when he got out. She walked towards him stridently. She was furious.

In person he was very tall and pencil slim. He wore a suit of some cheap, shiny material. Two children, a toddler and a little girl about seven or eight years old were in the back seat. Joy immediately disliked the man. There was something stiff and cold in his demeanor that was off-putting. And what was he doing speeding with two little kids in the back seat?

"Gaude Velasquez," he introduced himself. "Get out your insurance information," he instructed her.

Obediently, she went back to her truck and reached for her Hopeford card inside the glove compartment. Hopeford took only the best drivers. She had never had a moving collision in the fifty years she had been driving. Joy was incensed.

Gaude pulled out his insurance information. He gave her his driver's license number. She gave him hers. This exchange was not followed by any apologies or any caring as to how she felt. It seemed like a business transaction. There was something frigid and uncaring about this. Why didn't he apologize? He didn't even ask if she was O.K.

"Call me Gus," he smiled sleazily, and then whipped out his camera. He took several snapshots of his dented car. He seemed to be enjoying himself!

The quick work he was doing appalled her. Something was horribly wrong. The whole scenario seemed fishy. She had been going straight, driving with great care. Perhaps she *had* been going slow, but she'd been near the post-office where traffic moved slowly. He should have hit the brake instead of trying to pass.

The damage to his car was greater than hers. A dent followed from the middle of the passenger side door of his old car all the way to the tail-light that was smashed. Joy noticed that there was already a dent further forward, obviously made some time ago. It startled Joy that his camera came out so fast. It wasn't the type of camera one might carry in the glove compartment but a larger digital model. Joy blinked. She managed to gulp out a question. Actually, she was full of questions.

"What kind of car is this?" she asked.

"Oh, you know, a junk car, a Benz. It was your fault," he added.

"How was it my fault?"

"Intersection, you know. Coming out of the post-office like that, not looking."

"What do you mean? I sat there for several minutes until it was clear!"

"You must admit guilt. Say you are sorry. Say you are sorry."

"Of course I'm sorry." Joy was shaken and confused. How did it happen exactly? She couldn't think. She was in a state of shock. She only felt fear and confusion.

The little girl jumped out. She had been seated near the already dented side. Did she have a seat belt? Joy doubted it. There was a boy toddler strapped into a child's chair on the other side. He was quiet.

"Are you O.K.?" she asked the little girl. After rubbing her arm, the girl said she was fine. Gaude gazed at her proudly but said nothing. His silence about his children was peculiar. Didn't he care about them? She shuddered. A stab of fear shot through her. His callousness seemed inhuman. He seemed to be a very strange man: his icy stare shot through her. In all probability, the little girl was *not* fine. She might have some soft-tissue injury as she was seated right near the door and probably was banged against it.

"I'll take her to the doctor," Gaude blurted, as if suddenly realizing she may have been hurt. Still, he didn't seem very concerned. He hardly looked at his young daughter and, alarmingly, did not inspect her arm for damage.

Joy felt terribly uneasy and began to tremble. Something was terribly wrong with this picture. This Velazquez was too smooth, too business-like, too professional. He didn't really care about how his kids were; he didn't care how she felt. He didn't seem like someone who had just had an accident. His calmness seemed strange. A weird feeling came over her. She realized he scared her. There was something cruel about this man.

"You're shaking," he noted. He seemed somehow pleased.

"Yes, I am shook up." She just wanted to get away from him as quickly as possible. She sensed danger. This man was bad news.

He was too smooth, too clever. He seemed to have had practice at this sort of awful thing. Oh, God, what had happened to her? Exactly whom had she just encountered?

"I have to go home now," she told him. Joy glanced at her truck. There were some scratches and white paint but only on her bumper on the driver's side. Minimal damage to the hard black plastic. She would fix it herself with black shoe polish. It was nothing. Thank God she drove a truck! It protected her.

Joy did feel a little dizzy and her right knee hurt. It had received a jolt when her right foot on the gas pedal got knocked off. The knee had been slightly wrenched.

But she recovered from bruises and soft-tissue damage fairly easily. The swimming she did would get her through this pain. The main thing was that she had been going slow, probably less than twenty or twenty-five miles per hour, and no one was seriously hurt.

There was a witness, someone who had come out of his shop and was now standing watching them. Gaude went up to him. Joy skipped the interview. She just wanted to go home. She would regret this decision later.

Once at home Joy immediately called her insurance company, Hopeford.

"I came out of the post-office and rounded the corner past a big truck. This fellow tried to pass me but didn't have room and scraped against my bumper," she explained.

"You have to look when you come out of a post-office driveway. You have to be more careful," the agent chided her. The agent, Agnes, to her surprise, did not offer any sympathy. She was blaming Joy.

"But I *was* careful. There was no one coming when I pulled out. I waited several minutes in the driveway since I had to get around and past a big truck parked at the mailboxes. I was hit later when I was going straight."

"Well, you're liable. In this case, the post-office exit makes it your fault. The other driver had the right-of-way."

Joy was incredulous. Why didn't they believe her? There was absolutely no one coming when she exited the post-office. She had never been so sure of anything in her life.

"We're going to make a recording now of your statement. Is that O.K.?

"O.K."

"O.K. This is Agnes Maxim with Hopeford Insurance on July 13th, 2010. I'm speaking with Joy Bravitski regarding an accident that happened earlier today. Is this recording being made with your full knowledge and consent?"

"Yes."

"O.K. And if you can please state your name and spell your last name."

"Joy Bravitsky. J-O-Y B-R-A-V-I-T-S-K-Y.

"O.K." And you were the driver of the 2009 Chevy Silverado?"

"Yes, I, was. I am."

"Any damages?"

"No. Hardly anything, a few bumper scratches."

Any passengers with you?"

"No.

"O.K. Was anybody at all injured in the accident?"

"There was a little girl that was seated on the side where he hit my car."

"O.K. But was, was anybody injured that you know of?"

"She seemed fine." Joy wasn't sure she was fine, however. Hadn't Velasquez mentioned he would take the girl to the doctor?

"O.K. And what street and what direction were you traveling?"

"It's Old York, and I was going east."

"O.K. And how many lanes are there headed in the same direction that you were?"

"Only one lane. That's the problem."

"O.K. And how fast do you think you were traveling at the time of the incident?"

"I was going slow, under twenty miles per hour."

"O.K. When did you first see the other vehicle? About how far away was the other vehicle; a car length, less than that, more than that?"

"I didn't see the vehicle 'til after he hit me."

"O.K. And about…."

"I would say….."

"Hold on just a second. I got a few more questions."

"….and then let me tell you what happened."

"O.K."

"Now, what time of day was it when the accident occurred?"

"Around four-thirty or quarter to five in the afternoon."

"O.K. And what was the traffic like? Was it light, moderate, heavy?"

"Moderate. But the post-office is always busy."

" O.K. And if you can, just kinda describe to me what happened."

"Yes. I was coming out of the post-office, which has a very small parking lot, and I don't like to go in it as I consider it dangerous. I would never turn left out of that lot because it's too dangerous. There was a big truck parked right in front of the post office in front of the mailboxes so I waited until there was no traffic, and then I had to turn right slowly. I realize that anybody coming fast behind me would have to slow down for me because I have a big truck and I had to get around another big truck. So I did do a slow right turn. The car in back of me apparently…*I didn't see him…*was an old junk Mercedes." Joy was confused. Had she seen him? She couldn't think. Her brain felt paralyzed.

"O.K. When you say…hold on, hold on just a second. When you say the car behind you, were they behind you in the parking lot?"

"No, no."

"…or was he coming down the street?"

"He was coming down Old York, I guess." The accident refused to coalesce in her stunned brain. What had happened? Suddenly nothing she was saying made sense."

"O.K."

"…..at probably a, a very fast speed because I didn't see him." *Had she seen him?*

"O.K. And then what happened?"

"And then he….instead of slowing down and waiting for me to make my turn, he tried to pass me." This scenario made sense to Joy. This was how it happened, wasn't it?

"O.K now…."

"And he didn't judge, he didn't judge it right. There wasn't room…."

"O.K. But he, but he was on the street, though, correct?"

"Yeah."

"And you were pulling out of the parking lot."

"I pulled out. I don't know…."

"O.K. And what's the speed limit on Old York?"

"I think it's thirty or twenty-five, or something."

"O.K."

"I think he was speeding, and instead of slowing down, which he should have done, and waiting for me to make my turn, he tried to pass me. And there wasn't room. He didn't judge it properly. He was driving a junk car, in his words, an '82 Mercedes that was already dented on that side, so he has already misjudged…"

"O.K. But that has nothing to do with this accident. We...all we're gonna do is take into account what happened in this particular accident."

" So then, so then as you were pulling out, he came along. Then what happened?"

"I was just starting to gather some speed but not...I, I think I was going very slow. He, he...."

"O.K. Were you fully out of the parking lot at the time of impact?"

"Yeah, I was pulling out..." A confusion gripped her brain. Where did it happen? She couldn't think.

"What...was, was your vehicle...were you still pulling out of the parking lot..."

"No, no. I was pulled out and...""

"...or completely out on Old York?"

"I was next to the big truck." *But hadn't she gotten past the truck?*

"O.K"

".....when he clipped me."

"O.K. Old York."

"He clipped me, and he dented his side, which was already dented, and he blew his rear passenger- side glass bumper, whatever it is, light."

"O,K. So the point of impact on his vehicle, was it down the entire side or was it toward, more toward the rear ..."

"It's toward the rear. I would say."

"O.K....it's the last quarter."

"O.K. And where was the impact on your vehicle?"

"I'm missing some rubber on...I've got some white streaks on the bumper on the driver's side, but that's it. It's no big deal. A little shoe polish will fix it."

."O.K. And now were there any witnesses?"

"Yeah, there was a witness."

"O.K. Did they give you any information or anything?"

"No, they didn't."

"You talked to the witness?"

"No."

"You didn't see the other driver at all?"

"I'm a very careful driver, and I did make that turn very, very slowly and carefully to get around that truck."

"After the impact, what happened?"

"Well, I pulled over, and we exchanged information."

"O.K. And let's see. We have his insurance carrier as Allscrape. Is that correct?"

"Yes."

"O.K. And now, is there anything else you would like to add to the statement at all that we haven't gone over about the accident?"

"Yes. I just think Old York is a very dangerous street, that I've had this problem before, but I had never gotten hit, where someone will not let me in, will try to pass me on a one lane street. And it's very, very dangerous. I get very angry when they do that, because they're impatient."

"O.K."

"Like, once I was pulling out and the traffic was stopped, and I just went partway in, and the car behind me went around me instead of waiting for me to get all the way in on Old York."

"O.K."

"And I just think he was endangering his children. And he drove a junk car. He was traveling too fast. He didn't allow for the neighborhood post-office, where he knows there's going to be people going in and out. And he, instead of slowing down, he sped up and tried to get around me."

"O.K."

"And he didn't judge it properly. I think…"

"O.K."

"He was impatient and I don't feel this accident was at all my fault, although he tried to blame me for getting in his way."

"O.K. O.K. And have you understood all my questions?"

"Yes."

"O.K. And have your answers been true to the best of your knowledge?"

"Yes."…

"I hope this doesn't create a problem for my insurance, that it goes up because…"

"I couldn't tell you that. I only deal with the claim side of it."

"Yeah. I don't, I don't feel that…"

"O.K. Wait just a second. Let me get the…"

"…it's my fault at all."

"O.K. Hold on just a second. Let me get the recording off the line. I've got a couple more questions. Now, again, has this recording been made with your full knowledge and consent?"

"Yes."

"Thank you."

When Joy finally hung up on Agnes, she felt more confused and frustrated than ever. Somehow, it seemed, Agnes had tried to pin down this accident as being her fault! Joy felt somehow wronged. The questions had been good. But Agnes kept interrupting her. Joy had tried to make a point, the point being that it had not been her fault. But Agnes had steered the questions toward another direction. The pressure had been to make it seem as if she had failed somehow. Joy felt wobbly and confused. Had she failed?

No, Agnes was working for Hopeford. She would try to do what was best for the company. She would try to interpret the questions to her benefit. Agnes really didn't understand the accident at all. Joy wasn't sure she understood it either. But she was Hopeford's client. Shouldn't they have worked with her to get at the truth? She had been in a state of shock, in no position to figure out exactly what had happened. She had been honest and reported the accident immediately. Agnes gave her no credit for that or for being a loyal client for over twenty years. All this seemed most unfair. It rankled her that her insurance company was treating her like a felon!

She made up her mind to call Hopeford and to talk with Agnes's supervisor the next day.

The following morning she called Agnes. "I'm really confused about this interview I gave yesterday. I would like very much to talk to your supervisor."

"We consider it final. The initial interview is all that counts," Agnes replied.

"Let me talk to your supervisor," Joy demanded again.

"It's David Brenner. I'll put you through. His extension is 2365."

"This is David Brenner," a nicer voice stated.

"Hello. This is Joy Bravitski. I'm reporting an accident that happened yesterday afternoon shortly after four. I was coming out of the post-office but had already passed it and the big truck in front of the mailboxes. I had to wait several minutes until there was a clear road because I couldn't see well. A fellow tried to pass me. He didn't have room and careened against my front driver's side bumper. But I was past the post-office."

"When did you first see him? Where did he come from?'

"I don't know. He came out of nowhere."

"He must have come from *somewhere*. He must have been riding beside you at some point."

"I just can't remember any details." Joy was confused and in shock. "I remember I was afraid of him. I got all his information, though." She gave Brenner the man's name, driver's license number, his insurance company and policy number, and his phone number.

"We still need more details of how it happened. I know you are in shock. It may take a few days to come back to you. If you were hit coming out of the driveway, then we will pay him for damages and injuries. He would have had the right-of-way. We pay quickly."

"Oh, no! You must not pay him. You must not put me at fault and raise my insurance rates for three years. Look at my record. I've been with Hopeford twenty or thirty years and have been rated a superior driver most of those years. You think I would exit a driveway without looking? Not on your life!"

"Well, keep in touch. If you can find witnesses, it would really help. It's hard to prove that you were not at fault."

Joy hung up feeling helplessly frustrated. How could she prove that she had exited the post-office safely? Hadn't this Velasquez fellow tried to pass her? She had been going slow, cautiously going around the large truck. People didn't like getting behind her truck and often would try to pass her too close, cutting her off. But until now no one had actually hit her.

Why hadn't he slowed down? With two kids in his car, you'd think he would be more careful. He must have seen the post-office with people going in and out. Yet people did drive her street, Old York, a sleepy small-town section of two-lane road, as if it were a freeway. Some Hispanic men seemed jealous of her large, new truck. For a man, trucks were a status symbol, a masculine show-piece. Did her truck make him angry? He could have hit her on purpose, she supposed. But she dismissed this thought as absurd.

Joy needed to pack for her trip to Reno. She would think of other things, like her vacation, for instance. She would think about swimming, sunning, seeing her mother, all the great things happening soon. She would just brush off thoughts of insurance companies, inconsiderate, sloppy drivers, and misfortune in general.

She got out her maroon traveling satchel and began with two bathing suits. She would be swimming daily in Idlewild pool or Moana pool, the two pools where she had worked as a lifeguard in Reno. Her last piece of clothing was one dressy dress, a purple knit with a V-neck, for her mother's birthday party. After she was finished, she zipped up her satchel and breathed a sigh of relief.

Joy felt a little dizzy but perhaps her nephew Chris would do some of the driving and she could recoup her stability. She was very determined to forget this incident and just have some fun with her family. When Joy returned she would go to the doctor to find out if she had any serious damage. That could wait. Nothing too serious was wrong besides a few mild strains. Some aches and a few shooting pains when she climbed the twenty-five steps to her home. Swimming would take care of most of this.

Just some irritations, they would go away soon.

Chapter Five

Gus felt triumphant. He called Shortie.

"Shortie, I got a good one! A new Chevy truck with Hopeford Insurance. Driven by a woman, probably on the downhill side of middle-age. Probably paid for by her husband, or brother."

"Oh, you lucked out! Hopeford pays right away. Sometimes within the same week. And they pay well, I hear."

"Pretty easy work, if you ask me. She even said she was sorry as she was trembling like a leaf in the wind. I guess I scared the Hell out of her."

"She wasn't hurt, was she?"

'Probably some soft-tissue injury. I feel a bit achy and dizzy myself. And I had my kids with me."

"You know you shouldn't have done that! Your kids! They're too young."

"But I'll get more money."

"Still, it's bad. You can overcome aches and pains. But to do this to your kids? It isn't right, not right at all. It's different with Carlos. He's twelve."

"Well, we were going slow. Maybe less than twenty-five miles an hour."

"Still, Gus. Leave your little kids out of this!"

"We'll see. Juanita screamed but Juan was quiet. We'll get a good payment."

"Well, let me know when you get your check," he conceded. "We'll go out for a beer." He still sounded a bit upset.

"I'll probably be able to call you this week!" Gus didn't feel guilty at all. His kids would be fine. He had told the woman he hit that he would bring Juanita to the doctor. She seemed concerned about her. But he knew his girl would be fine in a month.

"See you," Shortie said. He sounded sad.

Gus hung up the phone. His wife worked for Senator Black as a receptionist and would be home within the hour. Maybe he would start dinner for the family. Gaude grabbed Juan and put him in his high-chair. Juanita could chop carrots. Jorge was reading *Alice in Wonderland*, and would be useless. He was a bookworm, not into food.

Gus would make a stew. There was some lamb in the meat keeper. He would sprinkle it with cumin seeds, sea salt and freshly ground pepper. He still felt on top of the world, ecstatic. So easy! Highway robbery made simple, he chortled.

He would call Mel Grant, his lawyer, in the morning. Mel always backed him up. Insurance companies were afraid of lawyers. They paid faster when he had a letter from an attorney claiming injuries. They were afraid of a big law-suit. Mel would get a fee for his work. There would be enough money to pay him. Easy money!

He would take Juanita and Juan to a doctor who would fill out forms and statements. He might even claim Jorge! This Joy woman was probably pre-Alzheimer's. She wouldn't remember if there were two or three kids in his car.

Not that Gus was overconfident but he had it all down pat by now. He might as well put his check in the bank tomorrow.

Velasquez prided himself on split-second timing, on-target aim, and risk-taking that took daring and sheer courage.

Moving up in the world was a goal. The Velasquez family's current home they only rented was a dingy white wood house encased in black steel guard bars. It was one street north of the main drag, running parallel to Old York, called Medway Street. With three kids and only two bedrooms, the little house felt cramped. It was also old and shabby. He deserved better, his taste running to clean, spacious, light-filled and contemporary. He deserved no less.

Gus had never revealed to his wife the nature of his profession. Instead, he told her he worked out of a warehouse with Shortie. He said he was the salesman and so wore his suit to work. Shortie sold auto-parts and he visited shops like AutoZone to sell product, he added.

Gus let her think he worked with insurance companies. Gus was vague about what he did for them but she had seen the checks. He was a convincing talker. Gus prided himself on his smooth delivery and how fast he thought on his feet. He never worried about persuading anyone. That Joy woman had even said she was sorry. He laughed out loud recalling this. And how her hands had been shaking! He must have really intimidated her.

Maria was coming into the house. Gus heard the door handle turn. She was still the Spanish beauty he had convinced to marry him. And it hadn't been easy. He had been sleeping with two other women when he knelt down on his knee to propose. There was Consuelo and Diana, both hot women with much to offer. They had beautiful bodies and luscious lips, long hair, and beautiful legs. He still felt some regret about renouncing them. Cheating on his wife was something he hadn't ever done, though he didn't completely rule it out for the future. He just needed to be richer to afford more than one woman. Women required money: restaurants, gifts like jewelry, hotels. He just couldn't afford extra-marital affairs at the moment, much as he would have liked to enjoy them.

But he turned off this train of thought as Maria entered the kitchen. She was a leggy beauty, her dark hair twirled up in a bun for work. It would come down later when he bedded her. He looked forward to the warmth of her olive skin against his.

"Smells good," she said with a smile. "Is this the lamb we got at the Super-A market last week?"

"Yes, in fact it is." He gave his wife a kiss on the cheek. Her face glowed with his affection.

"How are the kids? Did you take them to the park as you said you would after your insurance work?"

"We went to Eagle Park, right below the 134 freeway. There's a merry-go-round and a slide. The kids were jubilant."

"Did you do any work?'

"Yes, I worked for Hopeford Insurance Company. They pay quickly. I should get a check in a week or two."

"Well, I got so many compliments today on that ring you got me. Everyone in the office was gaga." She kissed him lightly. "I'll set the table. I see Juan is already in his high-chair. He's must be hungry."

Maria was smart, he thought, but she trusted him. Even though it was the wrong thing to do, he was glad she made that crucial mistake. A part of him wanted to tell her the truth about his insurance "work." He knew for sure that she would not like him injuring the kids. She would accuse him of not caring about them enough. No, he could never tell her. He would betray her trust as long as he could get away with it.

As they sat down to steaming bowls of stew Gus announced, "I'm taking the kids to the doctor tomorrow. Juanita was complaining about her arm. I think she bumped into something."

"How's your arm, Juanita?" Maria was concerned.

"Fine," her daughter said, rubbing her arm. Her daddy had said not to tell her mother about the accident and she obediently kept quiet about it. Probably Daddy was embarrassed. He was usually a good driver. She understood.

Juan, in the high chair, knocked over his milk which spilled all over the old carpeting. His hand had been shaking which was strange because he was usually a calm, stolid child.

"Oh, Juan," Maria chided. She got up to get a dishcloth and some paper towels to wipe up the mess.

"Juan's tired. He had a big day today at the park," Gus commented. "We'll put him to bed when he finishes his baby food."

"Give him a warm bath first," Maria advised.

"O.K., sure." Gus listened to what Maria wanted. She was the boss.

Bathing Juan, Velasquez thought about his day. Juan dutifully submitted to being scrubbed, only yelping in certain spots: his neck, his back, and his ankles. Yes, he had suffered some injuries but they weren't serious. Gus gave Juan his toy ducks so he could play and forget his pain. This worked well. The boy was quiet again.

He took his son out of the tub, wrapped him in a terry bath-towel, and drained the bathtub. Gus suddenly wondered if that Joy woman was O.K. He hadn't bothered to ask her. What did he care as long as he got her insurance information? She had really good insurance; that was all that mattered. He nodded as if agreeing with himself. He would forget all about her. Some dumb old broad, probably stupid, that happened to have a new truck. If she suffered, it was her own fault for being at the wrong place at the right time.

Anyway, she didn't matter, only the insurance reimbursement counted. She was just a pawn in his system. It could have been anyone coming out of that post-office. However, the fact that the truck looked new *did* matter. It was almost guaranteed to be insured. He would forget about her and just cash his check as soon as he received it. He should get it very soon. Anyway, she would recover from any slight injury. And he had hardly made a mark on her truck, only striking the bumper. How good was that! All in a day's work, he told himself, laughing. Still feeling ecstatic, he put Juan to bed.

Chapter Six

Joy greeted her nephew Chris as he came up the walk to her little home that was surrounded by Chinese Elm trees. She noticed his lanky good-looks, the easy way he had of carrying himself as if he hadn't ever been completely serious. But she knew he was very intense. He was a musician and played in the Pasadena symphony. All his free time was spent practicing the violin.

"Hi, Chris. Good to see you." Joy was genuinely glad. She liked her nephew, with his blondish hair and attentive blue eyes, very much

Joy was also happy that she had found the time to paint her front bumper. The black shoe-polish she bought hadn't worked as it was too transparent. But her black oil paint accomplished the job. You could still see gashes but the white paint streaks were gone and the marks weren't as deep as the oil paint filled them in a bit. Her bumper just looked a bit corrugated. Chris wouldn't even notice any difference. She could barely see it herself.

"I'll help carry your luggage down," he offered.

"Thanks. I only brought one bag but it's full," Joy replied.

They were soon on the road. Reno was a good eight or nine hours and they had agreed to start early at 6 a.m. She would drive most of the way but let Chris take over whenever she felt tired. That way, they wouldn't have to stop to rest.

She had asked Chris to help prepare a lunch and he brought chicken sandwiches on Italian panini bread. Joy packed home-made red-skinned potato salad plus fruit for dessert, in a thermal carrier. They would have a picnic in Lee Vining, where she liked to stop around noon or one whenever they reached the scenic spot. There was a park there with an old school-house overlooking the strange dead-looking Mono Lake. It really wasn't a beautiful lake, but the mysterious stillness of it enthralled her. She carried a quilt tucked in back of the seat for impromptu picnics like the one they were anticipating.

Joy had begun the trip intending to do most of the driving. But after they reached Palmdale and stopped to get a cold juice, Chris took over. Joy usually did not let others drive her truck but she still felt woozy and her ankle hurt when she held it on the gas-pedal for too long. Her knee also felt painful, and feeling that Chris was trustworthy, she allowed him to take over. She didn't tell him why. Joy was just grateful to have a driver. A chiropractor would help when she got back along with her swimming. This was just tempo-rary pain.

Getting past the Mojave Desert early was always a good idea in the summer. The announcer on the radio would predict the temperature to be a high of some boiling hot, unbearable degrees such as 112 or 120 in the shade. Sure enough, by the time they reached the desert, it was before eight and the temperature was already ninety degrees. She could feel the heat in her bones and her throat began to have a dry scratchiness.

As they drove through the Mammoth Lakes area, black clouds gathered over the massive mountains. Lightning and thunder cracked the sky and rain began pelting down in sheets. The wide, open space turned into a wet, dark fish-bowl. Joy was glad she had thought to bring the heavy waterproof tarp to cover her Art, which Chris had helped her pull over the works, before closing the folding cover. She felt comfortable in the warm truck as the rain poured down, assured that her art would be protected. Chris seemed to be enjoying the drive.

He switched the music on the radio from Classical Pops to Symphony Hall. Beethoven's dramatic music, his *Ninth Symphony*, filled the air, a stunningly appropriate accompaniment to the thunderstorm. A chorus swelled to the tune of the thunder. A perfect choral storm to the far off magnificent mountains, dazzling white snow still clinging to the highest peaks. Rain pelted down, slowly blurring the sky and clouds into a gray soupy fog.

Finally, when they approached Lee Vining, the sun reappeared like a goddess making an entrance. "We can still have our picnic overlooking the lake!" Joy announced smiling. The weather was dutifully cooperating.

Twenty minutes later, Chris pulled over and made a right to slowly find the park. Moments later, they found the serene spot. The grass was still wet but covering it with the quilt made it dry enough. The chicken sandwiches and potato salad were spread out along with bottled cranberry juice they had purchased along the way. A glorious picnic ensued. The sun felt warm and soothing on her aching muscles.

Joy gazed down at the deathly, mysterious lake below them as she munched the tasty sandwiches. The body of water had been produced by volcano-like geologic forces, and its waters were still and dark. The lake, almost black, was heavy with salt and very alkaline. No fish resided in the waters. Officials had brought fish once but they had not been able to survive. It was a dead lake, yet somehow existing. The bottom of the lake might be covered by deadly Arsenic. There was some controversy about that. Still some bacteria managed to survive and surprisingly some brine shrimp thrived on its toxicity. It was like the living dead. She felt mesmerized. A strange trance fell over her.

Suddenly Joy saw Gaude Velasquez staring at her as she gazed at the dead, saline lake. His dead, cold face seemed to float out from the surface of the glassy water. The whole "accident" began to roll through her brain like a film playing at a movie theater. She saw him aiming for her truck, purposely steering into it, sideswiping it with his tail- end. She saw his cold, calculating transaction, getting her insurance information. She saw him whipping out his camera. She saw his careless attitude toward the welfare of everyone involved, even his own kids.

"*I've been victimized*," she thought to herself. The realization that he had purposely, with intent, created an accident in order to cash in on her insurance policy was a rude shock. He had taken great risks with his children in the back seat!

She shuddered.

"Are you cold?" Chris asked. He volunteered his sweater, starting to remove it.

"No, I'll be fine. I just had a weird thought. This lake is forbidding."

"Yes, it does have a dead, creepy vibe about it. It's so still and dark."

"I guess we had better move on."

They picked up the quilt and folded it, then gathered waste to put in the trash, and Chris got behind the wheel and they continued the journey to Reno. But Joy's mood had turned sullen. She had decided to go to the police as soon as she returned to Los Angeles. Joy had met headlong, by accident, a cold criminal. By accident! A bitter laugh escaped her.

"What's so funny?" Chris asked.

"Oh, I was thinking about Mono Lake, how dead it is. That even fish died in it. Isn't it weird to find a lake with no living fish?"

"Yes, it is weird that the fish all died. It seems deadly, in a way. Yet the lake also has a kind of magic."

"Yes, it does hold a kind of fascination. But it's a cold, uninviting fascination like a crime story."

"People love crime stories!"

"They don't like crime stories when it happens to them, though. Being the victim is not enjoyable. You feel duped. Humiliated!"

"Yes, people don't like to be taken advantage of. I don't."

"I wonder why criminals persist. Crime doesn't pay. Everyone knows that."

"But some people think that they can get away with it."

"They must think others are stupid and helpless."

"Criminals are usually quite arrogant. They believe they have power over others."

"They like to pick on the vulnerable: children, old people. To have power over others, you have to be bigger, stronger, or believe you are more intelligent."

"I don't think crooks are very smart."

"But they believe they are. Smarter than their victim."

"I suppose it's a contest of sorts. Victimizing people takes a certain superiority complex. If the victim is aware of what's going on, that usually is the crook's downfall."

"That's a really good point, Chris. The victim might think it's just a mistake, for instance, if someone uses your credit-card numbers. It could be a mix-up, or it could be theft. If someone hits your car when you're driving down the street, it could be an accident or it could be an attempt to cash in on your insurance policy."

"Yes, staged accidents. I heard a whole family got killed that way when things went wrong."

Joy shuddered again. She was still in a state of shock. The realization that she had been in a staged accident, the staring, the cruelty to his own children, the chance Velasquez had taken when he was in the wrong lane, going the wrong way, all this stunned her. All she had gotten was some pain, some sore joints, and a bumper that was easily fixed with black oil paint. But Joy suddenly realized that she could have been killed had things gone horribly wrong.

For instance, what if he had hit someone going west when he was going east in the wrong lane? What if she had gotten inadvertently tangled up in a three or more car crash? What if he had encountered one of those big rigs or giant delivery trucks that often stopped at the store near her studio? Or a UPS or Fed-Ex truck that made deliveries everyday up and down Old York?

She could have been smashed to smithereens!

Joy looked over at Chris who was contentedly driving. Would this trip have even been possible? Would she never have had a chance to be at her mother's birthday party? She began to have feelings of hatred for this Velasquez man. How dare he try to risk her life? How dare he take this kind of chance? He could have also killed his kids if his plans had gone awry. Was he so desperate? He certainly had skills. He was a risk-taker, split-second timer, photographer, smooth talker. He had created this whole scenario, just as she created her Art. He was an artist of sorts: a con- artist.

He certainly had skills. He had created this destructive scenario, a "Happening," a negative, black event. A destructive creation, originating as an idea. Hitler had done it on a massive scale, killing her grandparents by starvation in the concentration camps. Osama bin Laden had done his 9/11 destruction utilizing airplanes to destroy the World Trade Center buildings in New York City along with most all of the inhabitants.

Joy had been having a show in Manhattan in SoHo when the World Trade Center tragedy happened. She had been only eleven blocks away. Her show had for all intent and purposes closed, though the gallery remained open. The one oil on paper that would have sold stayed in the gallery. The buyer was scared away. Trauma had haunted Joy in the past. Now it enveloped her once again.

Why couldn't he find a positive, helpful way to use his "talents," one that didn't involve hurting others? The risks he took were unacceptable. Didn't this man understand about karma? Whatever you do, the Buddhists believe, comes back to you. You might not see the results right away. But you *will* see them eventually.

But she must do the work when she got back. She must get a police report. Otherwise Hopeford would never believe her. The one witness in front of the store was, in all probability, not going to be around when she returned. She recalled the collision in precise detail now but what was lacking was proof.

Joy felt the worst thing was not that she would get her insurance rate raised for three years or receive a black mark on her driving record. The worst thing would be for Hopeford to pay off this cruel, cold criminal. A check from Hopeford would encourage Velasquez to continue his career in accident-staging. And the next victim might not get off as easily as she had. The next victim might get killed.

Chapter Seven

"Happy Birthday!" they all sang, some slightly off-key but with genuine emotion, as they smiled at Amy who sat proudly at the head of the table. Imagine someone looking so great and having so much energy and will to live at age ninety. Joy beamed. In her sixties, she still had her mother, though her father had died. Yet he had made it to the ripe old age of ninety-four. Now her mother had to find the strength to stand alone.

Amy's snow-white hair was carefully cut, like a cap around her head. Her brown eyes were wide with enthusiasm. Her tailored suit, neat and trim, reminded everyone of her years in fashion, creating clothes for her customers. Amy's creativity and exuberance, her taste and her fastidiousness, had contributed, Joy believed, to her mother's long lifespan. Amy always had goals, work, and something to look forward to. She walked around the park every morning, doing about a mile. She played bridge three times a week, keeping her mind as razor sharp as ever. On the phone she sounded fifty. She had always lived her life with exuberance and determination. A stronger woman would be hard to find.

Joy's brother, Gary, had rented a private room in a new, airy P.F. Chang's Chinese restaurant in Reno with its wood beams and tall windows. Shrimp, crab, lamb, noodles, brown rice with scallions, stir-fried vegetables, egg-rolls, bok-choy, one after another the dishes were brought in to be consumed with chop sticks. For dessert, Chris had found a Viennese bakery that had made a cake of thin layers of yellow fluff with marzipan and raspberry jam in between. Amy had always loved the ground almond marzipan she had grown up eating in Germany. It was her favorite sweet. The confection was frosted with whipping cream, another of mother's favorites. Whipped cream wasn't good for Amy's health, but it hadn't shortened her lifespan. Joy had not advised her mother against eating a fatty sweet she enjoyed so much. Enjoyment added to longevity also.

Joy reflected on having such a long life as she smiled at Amy. She had just had a close brush with what could have been death if things had gone wrong. How dare that Velasquez try to endanger her life! She thought again in horror of his criminal act. Just to collect on her insurance policy, he had risked the lives of his children and his victim. How dare he! She felt an urgency to get that police report. She fully intended to live as long a life as her parents.

How wonderful that Amy had adjusted so well to living on her own. She had been dependant on Ben for so much. She had never written a check. She had never learned to drive. Now she had to take the garbage out herself, wheeling the containers to the front for pickup. She had to learn how to handle the finances. She had to be strong at ninety. Of course, Amy had help. Once every two weeks, Terry, a part-time maid, came in to help clean and do heavy chores. A gardener came to take care of the lawn and fruit trees. Yet Amy picked the fruit herself: apples, peaches, pears, and red, juicy plums. Amy kept the home going on her own. Most of the work she did herself. Her strength amazed Joy.

For years Amy had talked about moving to a retirement home she had selected in the event her husband would die first. Her friend had moved there and enjoyed it. She would have her own room. Meals would be provided for her. She wouldn't have to cook or shop. They took residents on side-trips around the State. Joy's mother had even been anticipating the move.

But when Ben died, Amy found she couldn't part with the house she had lived in for over sixty years. Her clothes, many that she made herself, filled many closets. Giving them away was something she just couldn't do. Clothes had been her livelihood and her passion. Now Amy found she couldn't give up one of her joys of life. Moving to one room would mean giving up her furniture and rugs, her neat kitchen, her own bed. And she would have to pay thousands of dollars a month.

She had decided to stay home, in the house Amy and her father had watched being built when she was six years old. In this house, the one she had known so many years, she was content and happy. Amy was used to this house, so familiar and comforting. She would use the strength she had left over from a life of struggle and learn to cope on her own.

Joy had inherited some of her mother's strength. Yet she marveled at Amy's ability to adjust, to learn to run a household by herself. Gary took care of her taxes for her. The neighbors chipped in on driving her to the grocery store and keeping an eye on her. But Joy was blessed that Amy was not a burden. Amy took care of her own life, allowing Joy the freedom to take care of hers.

Life was precious.

"Pass the shrimp," Chris instructed, breaking her reverie. Joy complied, handing over the steaming dish. The joy and tranquility of the gathering filled her with contentment.

Life had not always been so comforting.

Joy remembered a conflicted household, full of heated argument, screaming and yelling. Her parents had fought constantly. Her dad had been possessed with an angry, violent streak and had started beating her at age six for any reason and no reason. His cruel streak only expressed itself in violence toward her. Otherwise, he was a quiet man. One never knew when an outbreak would occur. He terrified her when she noticed his rage beginning to gather. Joy knew she would get it. The resulting beating would be painful and traumatic. She would cry for hours.

As a result, Joy had become afraid of people. Her world as an artist offered the solace of spending a great deal of time alone. She liked being alone; it comforted her.

Most people couldn't stand the amount of time she spent by herself. Having an assistant did break up some of that aloneness but her career had hit the skids. She could not afford an assistant now, except occasionally.

For years, Mickey had worked for her. Then it was Val, a Mexican. Val was a hard worker who could figure out answers to most problems Joy encountered. He was very clean and knew janitorial work. He painted the studio, built an awning for the back door so the rain didn't come in, and re-stacked the paintings so they did not dig into each other. He could build anything, fix anything. He had a huge ego, however, and couldn't take any instruction. He wanted to be left alone to figure it out for himself. If she offered a helpful tip, he would scoff at it, ridicule it, before he rejected it. Val had to be the one in charge. Sometimes it seemed she was *his* assistant and she was working for him!

Yes, Latino men wanted to be in charge. They leaped at a chance to belittle and sublimate women. Once in a while she had had to dismiss Val. She just couldn't take his brow-beating. And yet she always took him back. There was always a reason to call him again. He had been invaluable to her, even when she cut his hours to a couple of days a week. She knew the problems that would come up at the studio, the deliveries that had to be made, the construction of stretcher bars, the sizing and priming of canvas, the finishing of the edges with three coats of gesso, the wire to hang the work, all this could not be so easily accomplished without Val. And he was especially good at studio organizing, maintenance and repair. He could handle any emergency and was quickly available. He came on time and was a reliable assistant. She had learned to put up with his macho one-upmanship. He worked hard. After twenty-two years, however, he found a full-time job. Her career had slowed to the point that she couldn't give him enough hours.

Now her nephew Chris worked for her once in a while. He was the best stretcher-builder she had ever had. He was a delight to work with. Yet he was overqualified with his degree from the

University. He had his music to practice. He also had a part-time job. It was not always easy to get him over. She always felt she should pay him more. But sales now were so sporadic. She was lucky to have him come to the studio to help her occasionally.

Joy glanced over at her niece Bridget, who was pregnant with her first child. Amy would soon be a great-grandmother! Amy beamed at Bridget. Bridget's eyes glowed back with pride. She had quit her office job working for MGM studios and moved to San Diego where she had found Greg. The two had gotten married in a glorious sea-side wedding. Now Bridget would soon be a mother. Joy was ecstatic. She had helped Bridget move south even though it had been raining that day. Bridget felt the move was urgent. She hadn't wanted to wait even a day or two for the weather to cooperate. She was right. Her destiny was waiting.

Joy helped Chris cut the cake. Each slice seemed like a celebration. "My favorite!" Amy exclaimed. "You went to too much trouble for me. But I'm enjoying all of this so much!"

Joy was proud of her growing family, even though she had never had children. Everything had been forsaken for her art. She dated but marriage had seemed like something that bound her into a role that would not suit her. She needed her freedom to devote her time and energy to her painting. After a day working on large canvases, she would return home exhausted. Even with an assistant to help, the energy required for a seven or eight-foot canvas depleted her. Now Joy also did all the assistant work herself. And the sales work too as she had no galleries to do it for her now. Galleries would come again and take the load off her. She knew it would happen. But when?

There were always other things to take her time and energy besides painting. For instance, the police report. She needed to get one in a hurry. There was no time to waste. Gaude Velasquez might be driving around right now with his children in the back seat- his toddler, his brave little girl- looking for his next victim. She shrugged off this thought as she passed egg-rolls to Chris.

The main thing was being there to celebrate Amy, her long life, her triumph over the hardships of living.

"You made it through all the problems and the trouble Gary and I gave you," she complimented her mother.

"I don't know how I did it all. But I know one thing: all the trouble was worth it."

"You are the strongest person I know," Joy acknowledged.

"You inherited that strength. No one can tell you anything."

"That's true," Joy agreed. Everyone laughed.

Joy did have time in Reno to make an appointment at the one good gallery. Some of her friends showed there. She really liked the owners Patty and Don.

Arriving, she pulled the paintings out of the back of her truck, carrying the work into the gallery and lining it up against a back wall. Joy held her breath. Patty liked the work but the director did not seem to be in a hurry to take anything.

"You can have one of the works for a year on consignment," Joy volunteered after a long silence. "Which one would you choose?"

Patty hesitated. Finally she picked the best one, a recent small canvas loaded with color. "Your color sense is your best asset," she noted, picking up the canvas and taking it to her office. Patty wrote up a consignment sheet for the canvas titled *Marine Slick.*

Joy breathed a sigh of relief. Though it didn't mean any money yet, she could bring her mother to see it. Amy was into success. She would be pleased to see Joy's progress.

The next day Joy brought Amy to see the canvas at the beautiful, modern gallery. Patty pulled out her painting.

"I like it," Amy said. Joy felt a rush of relief. It wasn't easy for Amy to understand or appreciate abstract Art. Amy liked "realism." Most people needed Art to resemble something they actually knew. They wanted Art to look like a photograph.

Joy felt her trip had been a success on so many fronts. It was important that Amy see progress in her Art career. Her parents had been against the idea of her choosing to be an artist. Becoming an artist had been an uphill battle. *Being* an artist became a continuation of that struggle. Coming up with strong, competent, even great work was a daunting challenge. However this wasn't enough. To survive, the paintings and drawings had to sell. And the sales had to be continual. That was the hard fact of being an artist. In order to stay in the studio all day doing painting and drawing versus getting a job(something she had been told to do during her whole career by well-meaning relatives), one had to sell the work produced. And it simply had to be good enough. The trip had given Joy an interlude from the treadmill pace she had been on for so many years.

Her wonderful and dramatic drive to Reno with Chris, the realization of what had happened to her in the "accident," the glorious birthday party, and now her foot in the door at this prestigious gallery, all contributed to a successful trip.

Joy would go back to Los Angeles feeling her mission was accomplished.

Chapter Eight

Checking her mailbox on returning home, Joy saw a letter from Hopeford.

"You have been found over fifty-one percent liable for the accident on July 13, 2010. You have thirty days to dispute this finding. If you disagree, send a letter of dispute to Hopeford within the next two weeks."

Immediately, Joy called Hopeford. "You are more than fifty-one percent liable," Agnes, who answered, told her defiantly. You are one-hundred percent at fault. You came out of the post-office without looking. We reviewed photos of the damage and that's what it is."

"No! That's not what happened. I wasn't hit at the post- office. I came out when it was clear. I was hit further up the road. The post office is near Avenue 51. I was hit near Avenue 52."

"Well, you would need a witness. We don't change our decision."

"I'll look for one."

"Let us know right away. We hear both sides of the story. Velasquez says you hit him at the post-office when he obviously had the right of way."

"He's a liar!"

"Well, it's a case of he says, she says. Without a witness, we can't remove your liability."

"I'll go to the police."

"That might or might not help. And our judgment is final."

"The truth will come out. The truth will win."

"Well, let us know if you find any witness."

"Why am I guilty until proven innocent?" she demanded.

"That's just how it works here," Agnes bluntly stated. "I have a medical appointment now and I have to go. Sorry."

Joy hung up feeling frustrated and angry. How dare they think she hit only his rear side at the post-office! If she had hit him there, wouldn't it have been strange to have seen the front end of his car go past her and then hit his rear side? She would have had to be blind! And how could she have made such a gash going one or two miles an hour? A deep dent like that could only be made by a car going almost twenty miles per hour, the rate of speed she had been driving. It didn't make any sense.

"The insurance company wants to do what is expedient," Carey explained when Joy called her later. "They want to pay him off quickly, get rid of it, and charge you more money for three years. In effect, you pay for the accident with the increased charges on top of your regular bill. They are in business to make money. They don't want to be sued by his lawyer. Lawsuits are expensive."

"But how can I prove it? The witness has gone to South America, his son told me. He won't be back for at least six months. I went up and down Old York. Across the street at the auto repair shop, there is a video camera aimed at the street. But it only keeps film for one week. I was in Reno for my mother's ninetieth. I'm too late to find the video."

"Try the police. It's your one chance to prove you are innocent."

"Did Stan ever show up?"

"Yes he did. We went to Santa Barbara and had a wonderful weekend. We took a picnic to the beach for supper and watched the sun sink. So romantic! I do love that guy. Even though he's hardly ever around, it's worth the wait. I explained your situation to him and he called it 'Cash for Crash.'" He also thought the guy might be 'hitting on you.'"

Joy laughed. "Cash for Crash! That's exactly what it was. He really got it. Thank him for me for the hundredth time for making me laugh again. Velasquez is probably married with those children. He's not my type. I don't think he would give a fig for my company. He wanted my insurance card. Guys used to stare intensely at me the way he did. But they don't now. I'm too old."

"You still look good, don't kid yourself. But I agree he was trying to cash in on your insurance policy. How is that going?"

"Oh, my insurance company still doesn't believe me. I'm going to the police tomorrow. And I've written a letter to Hopeford, as they requested, to dispute their findings."

"Well, good luck. I hope you convince them to write a report that will demonstrate your victim-hood. You were set up. You had nowhere to go to avoid him."

"Yes, I tried to speed up. But just as I had that thought, he careened in front of me. There was no escape. It was as though he read my mind. And I wasn't quite at the next intersection to make a quick turn right. I was just in the wrong place at the right time."

"Well, there was nothing you could have done differently. Best just not to worry too much about it, though I know you will. Stan says hello. He'd like us to get together with you soon."

"I'd like that. Tell him I liked his jokes."

"Ciao for now."

Joy had an idea. If she had been hit at the post-office, the clerks would have seen the accident. The post-office fronted the street. It had large plate-glass windows that allowed full, unobstructed views of the driveway and street directly in front of the building. She would type up a statement and ask one of the clerks to sign it.

Arman was working at the counter at the post-office when Joy went in the next afternoon. He was happy to sign the statement she made up for him. "I saw nothing," he said. "I was working on the thirteenth of July. If there had been a crash, I would *definitely* have seen it. There is no doubt, whatsoever. There was no crash directly in front of the post-office."

Joy was sure this was proof. If there was no accident directly in front of the post-office seen that day, how could Velasquez have hit her there? It just made perfect sense.

But this did not convince Hopeford. "We need a witness that saw what exactly happened. Having a witness that saw nothing doesn't count," Agnes' sour voice intoned.

"But if the accident did take place in front of the post-office, Arman would certainly have seen it. He faces the street and he can see both the driveway and the road in front very clearly. The collision made a loud, awful screeching noise. He was working that day. Arman knows me and would certainly remember if he had seen my truck in a crash. And he definitely would have heard it."

"I'm sorry, but we still need a witness who saw the crash, not one who didn't see it." Agnes wouldn't budge.

Joy felt stuck. Still there was the police. She would gather her courage and go to the Police Department in the morning.

The next morning, bright and early, Joy went to the nearest police department on the edge of Glendale. The officer who was about to take the report was Hispanic. Joy felt her chances of getting anywhere with him were dim. The chances this macho officer would take her side were slim to non-existent.

"You had an accident," Valverde noted, taking information down on a pad.

"Yes, I did come out of the post-office. But I was past it, going straight, when Mr. Velasquez hit me. He was going the wrong way, going east in the west-bound lane."

"Let me see the damages."

"My truck is out front. But I painted over the driver's side bumper where he hit me." Joy started to go out with him to show the truck.

"Let me see it alone," he instructed, his macho need for control exerting itself.

Joy waited inside the old police station. It had a dingy look. On one wall was an ATM from a Credit Union. People popped in to use it. Against another wall, officers were drinking coffee and shooting the breeze. Finally, Valverde came back in.

"I saw where he hit you. I'll write it up as a report but I'm going to have to put down that it was *your* fault." He smiled triumphantly.

"Thank you very much but that would not be the truth. Is there someone else I can contact?"

"You can go downtown to Central Traffic. But you must take this note with you."

He proceeded to write a note explaining that it was her fault.

Joy grimaced. She took the note and thanked him again. He had given her directions to Central Traffic. It was already 10:30. The day seemed to be shot as far as doing anything creative. She might as well drive downtown. Joy was angry. Valverde, with his smug smile, seemed only to want to give her a hard time.

Central Traffic was located in L. A.'s garment district. Joy passed storefronts in front of which colorful dresses, skirts, blouses, and pants were hung outside, hoping to pull in customers. Here and there were shoppers looking in the window or carrying bags full of their purchases. There didn't seem to be anywhere to park so she took the loading zone. Her truck made it possible to park in these types of spaces.

The officer in charge was Hispanic once again. Joy winced. However, he did not fit her preconceived notion and seemed sympathetic. Joy decided not to start her story with the post-office this time. She would begin her story where she was actually hit.

"I was going straight," she told Hernandez. "The street had only two lanes, one going east and one west. I was going east. A fellow next to me, Velasquez, was going the wrong way parallel to my truck, going east in the west-bound lane. He was staring at me like a race-car driver sizing up his competition. Suddenly, he switched lanes, smacking the front bumper of my truck with his rear passenger side. I think he did it deliberately to collect money on my insurance policy. When I saw he was going the wrong direction in the wrong lane, I thought he was a weirdo and tried to speed up. But he fish-tailed and hit me before I had a chance."

"It wasn't your fault," Hernandez noted. "You were in a staged collision, a sideswipe, is what we call it. I'll write it up. We need your registration and insurance card."

"I'll go get those. They're in my truck," Joy said jubilantly.

Joy went outside feeling victorious. She reminded herself not to pigeon-hole Hispanic men. Los Angeles was inundated with Latino people. Sometimes it felt as if she were living in Tijuana.

"Move your truck, lady! We had a delivery and there wasn't a space for the driver! You should be ticketed and towed!" A garment- district store owner was furious at her, waving his fist.

Joy apologized. She would have to find another space which would take time. Would the officer, Hernandez, think she disappeared? Fortunately, there was an empty space in the next block. This one had a meter. She fished around for her registration and insurance card, put money in the slot, and went back to the station. Hernandez seemed a little worried, though he had begun writing up the report.

Joy felt a rush of relief. The cranky Agnes woman at Hopeford told her a jury would judge her liable for coming out of the post-office. But a jury would weigh a police report heavily. A jury would tend to side with the police, an official agency, over a fishy version that was told by Velasquez. His smooth sales-pitch would fall flat compared to an official police report.

"You can get this report next Friday," Hernandaz told her. He pointed to a room opposite his counter. "That's where the reports are written and officially stamped. Meanwhile, you can talk to Detective Marion Miller. She's in charge of the Auto-Fraud Investigation Department. Here is her phone number. Call her immediately."

"Thank you very much. I will follow through," Joy said, leaving the station with Detective Miller's phone number clenched in her hand.

Won't Velasquez be surprised when he doesn't get his money! She felt triumphant. The consequences Joy might face for his disappointment did not occur to her. If he was a sore loser, she figured he would be angry. But that was the extent of her concern.

Most of all Joy felt jubilant as she headed back to her truck, then to the freeway to drive back to the studio. Joy would have her bagged lunch and then have the whole afternoon to paint. Once in the studio, she also made an appointment with a sports injury doctor down the street. He could write a report. Hopeford said they would cover her treatment. She was covered for ten thousand dollars but doubted she would go more than once. This was not an expensive injury.

Her swimming had taken most of the pain away already, just as she had expected.

Chapter Nine

"Your tendons and ligaments and the surrounding tissue in your leg were bruised and wrenched," Doctor Clark said as he massaged her knee with some cream. He put an electrical instrument on her leg. Her limb felt warm as it massaged the muscles.

"It's called soft-tissue injury and it happens when your body is wrenched in a different direction than it is aimed at. Auto accidents and sports injuries are the prime cause."

"How long will it take to heal?"

"You should be free of pain in a month. You can come back once a week if you want."

"I do a lot of exercise, swimming and weights. I'll probably be O.K. with just this one visit. I need a report for my insurance company."

The office was small and sparsely furnished. Nevertheless, Joy felt Dr. Clark knew what he was doing. She felt better already. And she would have evidence that she was injured. Joy was doing everything possible to prove she was telling the truth to Hopeford. She needed to be credible. The fact that they didn't believe her was still a hard pill to swallow.

Back at the studio, Joy also called the DMV to report Velasquez as a dangerous driver.

"We have a form you can fill out," the clerk informed her, "a request to have him reexamined for his driver's license."

"Yes, please send that to me. I'll fill it out and return it."

Joy felt she was in some sort of fight, some power-struggle with Velasquez. He was trying to put the blame on her. The tension she felt against him was unexplained, as she had never seen him again. However, the phantom of a fight hung in the air as she matched her wits against him.

The Internet had also revealed a National Insurance Hot Line. She had called them, explaining the situation. To her surprise, they were sympathetic.

"There was an accident staged on the Long Beach Freeway by a man in a lightweight car. He aimed at a truck. Not the smartest maneuver. He was smashed to unidentifiable pieces. The truck driver had the same problem you have. His carrier did not believe his story. He lost his job. Then he hired a private detective agency who found out this fellow that hit him had been in other staged accidents. The truck-driver got his job back. It's characteristic in these cases to cast doubts on the victim. That's what is so hard. Not only do you get injured but you are charged as the guilty party." The woman who related this tragic story was informative and kind as well as empathetic.

"Well, thanks for your sympathy. I feel relief just talking to you."

"Take care of yourself."

Joy felt better. Several things had lightened her mood: Stan's humor, finding a police officer that actually believed her, a chiropractor who knew how to help soft-tissue injuries, and then Hopeford giving her another month to prove her innocence. She had enough of a financial struggle without having her insurance premium raised every month. Besides, Joy didn't want the DMV thinking she was a sloppy driver when actually she had been extra-careful that day.

Velasquez would be angry. She had done several things to thwart him, Joy knew. He would be upset about not getting paid. He would be exasperated at having to take a driver's license test all over again.

The police had given the report to the detective, Marion Miller, who would investigate Velasquez and his driving practices. If he was proved guilty, he might even go to jail for using his vehicle as a weapon to collect money.

The next morning she talked to Detective Miller over the phone.

"Accident-staging is difficult to prove. The D.A. needs uncontestable proof. You don't have a witness, which is doubly difficult. Nevertheless, we have his driver's license number and we can make sure he doesn't do it again. If the kids are in danger, we can report him to the Child Endangerment Authorities. They may have to remove the kids from his home."

"It might be the best. He seems to be a cruel father."

"Accident-staging is usually done by one person. We don't usually see this criminal type intently injuring his children. You met up with the rotten apple in the barrel."

"Just my luck! Well, thanks for your investigation. It makes me feel a whole lot better. It's a great relief to have someone to talk to who is sympathetic!"

"Stay well. Please do keep in touch. I need to have all the details you can remember or anything that subsequently happens that is relevant to the case."

"Will do." Joy felt a tremendous rush of gratitude as she hung up the phone. This horrific incidence had been a burden that she had carried around with her since July 13, and the burden was doubled by the fact that Hopeford didn't believe her.

A week later, Joy had plans to get together with Carey and Stan for dinner. She searched her closet for something celebratory to wear. Bright colors and bold accessories seemed to be called for. She picked a bright blue tunic-sweater to wear with her Calvin Klein jeans, accessorizing the outfit with the turquoise necklace and bracelet Bridget had sent for her birthday.

Joy dressed feeling almost giddy to be alive and well. Her aches and pains were healing. Her knee no longer felt a stab of pain when she climbed the stairs to her home. Her ankle had also mended to the point that she could drive without feeling her foot giving out. The chiropractor said it would take a month. Had she been fighting for that long? Velasquez still hadn't gotten any money. Joy felt his fury, though she had no contact with him.

For over a month there had been a blackness to Joy's life that she couldn't shrug off. The evil intent, the intent to harm, hung over her like a storm cloud ready to burst torrents of hail. Joy couldn't encounter a criminal, however inadvertently, without it affecting her daily life. The cruelty he had displayed had cast a spell on her. Joy felt terrified at times when she was driving straight ahead. She looked constantly in her side mirrors and turned her head to see who was driving right next to her, like a bank robber making a getaway. She was frightened in traffic; an encapsulating fear and wariness took hold of her that she had never experienced before.

Driving suddenly became an acutely dangerous habit she was addicted to. No longer did it seem like a normal activity. Now Joy felt vulnerable and paranoid whenever she took the wheel. She suddenly realized that it was not enough to be careful, to obey the traffic laws, to stop at stop signs and red lights, and to obey the speed limit. Now she had to watch out for victimizers trying to crash into her! As if there wasn't enough to be wary about when taking the freeway or cruising the dangerous streets of L.A.

Joy was acutely aware that she had lost some of her freedom—the freedom to drive with pleasure and confidence. Velasquez had smashed that feeling of freedom forever. It had been replaced with a feeling of terror. Now the crazy streets of L.A. had become a looming threat.

Nightmares haunted her. She would wake up with a start after being crashed into, enveloped in a Technicolor nightmare, though the car that hit her was always dirty white. Eyes would stare at her when Joy drove her truck though the dream; they were always Velasquez's eyes. He was staring at her with intent to kill. She would wake screaming, believing that she had been crashed into or shot.

She had felt haunted as though being stalked. Her life had changed forever.

Joy was in desperate need of a fun night out with her friends.

Meeting Carey and Stan at the Mexican restaurant helped her immediately. Just gazing at her friends gave her a rush of relief and anticipation.

"Joy, you look terrific," Stan complimented her. "Let's get a table and commiserate." Stan walked up to the reservation desk. "Table for three," he requested. He was a large man, part Cherokee Indian. His dark, glossy hair had turned stark white. He still wore it longish around his round ears. His large nose dominated a full face with a bit of mirth at the corners of his mouth. He was a stand-up comedian who had done some acting. There might be a movie coming up soon where he could display his talents. Stan's body was athletic and he moved with fluidity and grace. His large hands were always gesturing as he spoke, usually with great enthusiasm and vigor. He was popular with all ages and a bit of a celebrity. He could make anyone laugh, even the stodgiest of men. He could probably even make sour-voiced Agnes at Hopeford Insurance break down in laughter, Joy thought, smiling. Or would that be possible?

They were shown to a booth in the corner. The waiter set down a big bowl of taco chips and a small red clay bowl of thick guacamole for them. Then water glasses were set down. Joy grabbed a chip, dipped it in the smooth, green avocado and put it into her mouth. A sensation of cool, green luxury came over her.

"So what's it like to fight with Hopeford?" Carey asked. She was also dressed in designer jeans but paired them with a raspberry red cashmere turtleneck sweater. Her blonde hair was long and hung to her back. Her face was animated, her intelligent blue eyes were accentuated with long lashes.

"Hopeford? Hopeless," Joy laughed, grabbing another taco chip which were becoming addictive. "Well, no. When I gave them the police accident report number, things changed. But I couldn't get the actual report on Friday as I was told by Officer Hernandez. When I called on Thursday, they told me I had to request the report and send a check for twenty-three dollars. It takes twelve weeks to get it!"

"Twelve weeks! I guess that will stall this case for them!" Carey reached over to Stan, giving his arm an affectionate squeeze.

"They are changing their mind, I think, but rather slowly. They want to send a detective out to interview me." A waiter appeared with tomato and red onion salads.

"Really? Stan chimed in. "That is really a turnaround. Guess the police scared them worse than the lawyer!" He dug into his salad with gusto.

Joy laughed. "They're worried about being sued. The jury might decide I got hit coming out of the post-office. But the police report says 'Sideswipe by staged collision' so that would carry enough weight, I suppose, to convince a jury I was not at fault."

"Not to change the subject," Carey interjected, "but how is the art coming along?" She was finishing her salad. The waiter then brought enchiladas loaded with spicy green sauce. Carey's eyes widened and she picked up a fork.

"Oh, great! That's the one variable in my life that doesn't vary. In fact when I have tension in my life, it makes the paintings stronger."

"I don't see how they could be much stronger," Stan observed. "They knock your socks off as it is." He dug into his enchilada with gusto.

"Thanks Stan. But I know they can always improve. With each painting, I know a little more about color, composition, balance, light-and-dark, and how to make the thing work!" Joy licked her lips. The tomato salad had slipped down easily. She was ready for the enchilada that glistened in front of her.

"They always work," Carey chimed in. "Not like my screenplay. I throw out a lot of writing effort."

"Oh, we're in the same boat," Joy countered. "I throw out a lot of work too."

"Do you really? I'd like access to your trash," Stan joked.

They all laughed as the waiter brought more orders of tamales surrounded by rice and beans. Stan had also ordered strawberry Marguerites all around.

As they dug into their repast, Joy was thinking how great it was to have friends. Her friends made a huge difference in her life. They were a treasure she was so fortunate to have! Stan liked to leave funny messages on her caller I.D. She would print up the caller I. D. report on her home phone and find that she had been called by "Unavailable," "LA FOP LODGE 1" or "THNK SAY ACT 10," or "YOUR LOCAL CONT." When Stan wanted a call from Joy, he would leave a "message" which consisted of an operator informing her that "her call did not go through. Would she please try her call again?" This message was followed by assorted, irritating noises: busy signals, taped crowd noises, or the horrible, grating noise the phone makes when left off the hook, played horribly loud. This caused her to cringe, then laugh. Although he was Carey's boyfriend, Stan kept all of his friends laughing with his pranks. He was flirtatious with women who caught his eye, always ready for conquests.

Joy had never confronted him. However, she knew it was him and usually she would call him back. His secretive nature created a mysterious persona. And he kept Carey in the dark. Did he love Carey? It certainly seemed to Joy that he doted upon her. But Carey said he never told her or admitted his feelings. He also would not commit to her. Carey accepted this with a shrug. Pressuring him didn't work, she had learned the hard way. He just ran off. Stan even dated other women.

"I don't know if I would want to marry him, anyway," she would rationalize. But Joy thought Carey would if Stan ever did get around to asking her.

Stan picked up the check. "Thanks," Joy, said. "That was wonderful Mexican food. I'm turning into a Latino. When I go to the corner grocery store to get my afternoon cranberry juice, I always say 'Muchas gracias!'"

"Well, gracias to you for your company. It's a pleasure to have a great artist to dinner!" Joy returned the compliment with a grin.

"Thanks again. It's a pleasure to know a great comedian!"

They all laughed. "I'll call you tomorrow," Carey told Joy.

Chapter Ten

" I don't get it, Mel. It's over three weeks and there is no check in the mail," Gaude complained to his lawyer. "Hopeford Insurance pays right away. There must be a hitch. I don't know anything about this broad I ran into, but she didn't seem much of a fighter. A skinny, shaking, fearful wisp!"

The two were seated in Mel's sleek office in downtown Los Angeles in a crisp, modern building on the seventeenth floor. Below, the tangle of streets, soaring high-rise buildings, office-workers scurrying to their next assignment, lawyers hurrying to their court dates, and shoppers carrying bundles, provided a stim-ulating view.

"I'll write a letter to Hopeford explaining that three kids were hurt, besides your own injuries. That'll move things along. You should have a check next week. Insurance companies want to set-tle fast. Court cases are long, drawn-out and expensive."

"Thanks, Mel. I need the money. I took the kids to the doctor. Juan and Juanita have soft tissue injuries. They will need physical therapy for several weeks. I have injuries too. But I can bear pain better than they can. Jorge was home but you might as well claim him too. I can rough him up a bit. Take him to the doctor next week. This Joy broad was too shook up to count kids, though she did ask if Juanita was O.K. when my girl jumped out."

"You'll have a bigger check with three kids. We might as well go for it. But take it easy on Jorge. He's a good kid."

"I'll just beat him a bit, maybe use his baseball bat. Not too hard. Just a few bruises. I need the money. I'm going to junk that junk Mercedes and get something a little safer. That car looks like a colander!"

"Well, let me know when you receive the money. It should come soon."

Gus, after saying thanks to Mel, walked to the elevator. He felt reassured. Mel was a cracker-jack attorney. The insurance companies were intimidated by him. Velasquez had perfect confidence that Mel would be able to get him his check. There was no doubt in his mind.

He found his car easily in the parking lot. It stood out in a sea of shiny, clean new automobiles.

Once home, Gaude called Shortie to vent his frustration. "Shortie, I still haven't gotten paid from Hopeford."

"That's really weird. They usually get right on it. They are the most efficient company. If there is a problem, I'm sure they will fix it."

"How's Carlos doing?"

"He's recovered from our last escapade. He's doing very well in school. Got an A in English!"

"That's great! And Rosie?"

"She just joined a gym. You know she needs to lose at least thirty pounds. She's determined to get her figure back."

"Too many tacos!"

"Yes, she does like to eat. And she's a very good cook, I must say."

"Well, there's no reason to celebrate here. Mel is writing a letter claiming three kids were injured. A letter from an attorney is alarming to insurance companies. They get scared and pay fast.

Court cases cost big money. Maybe we *should* go to court. I'm not letting that broad off the hook. She must be blocking the payment somehow. I can't figure it out. Insurance companies like to settle quickly."

"Maybe you underestimated her. Do you know anything about her?"

"The woman wasn't bad-looking but she was wearing old, painted- up clothes."

"Maybe she's an artist. There are lots of creative types in that area."

"She was thin, maybe skinny even. A fly-weight. She's probably causing this confusion. I'm getting angry. I need the money and was counting on it. I can't take the kids out for another collision right now. I need another car. I have to pay out-of-pocket for the doctors' bills. I have to compensate Mel for his time and letter-writing. The kids need time to get well."

"Well, just wait it out. I'm sure you'll get a fat check soon."

"I'll call you as soon as I get it. We'll go out for a beer."

"Sure thing. Good luck."

Gus got up and went to his mailbox. As he pulled the letters and bills out of the mailbox, his glance caught at the DMV return address. What did they want? He felt alarmed, as if a shrill fire bell had gone off. He rapidly tore open the envelope.

"You are required to report to the Department of Motor Vehicles for re-examination of your Driver's License. You have until August 31 to report to your local office," it stated.

Gaude's face turned red with humiliation and anger. So the *muchacha* was up to her tricks, was she, the bitch? She was making big trouble for him. Why didn't she just cooperate? It was her fault he wasn't getting his money! Meanwhile, his bills were piling up. There was one from the DWP. The electric and water department had raised the rates. It was shocking how much they charged. And Maria did not get much for her salary. He felt Senator Black took advantage of her.

Reluctantly, he called the DMV to make an appointment. He must look sincere. Better to get it over with. Still, he was angry. Who did that woman think she was putting him in this embarrassing position? He would take his driver's test all over as if he were sixteen years old! He would be able to go Friday, August 28. They weren't taking appointments for that day, he found when he called. He would just have to show up and wait in line. When Gus put the phone down, he picked up the bills and threw them against the wall in fury. He would like to eliminate this Joy woman. She was putting him through Hell. "I'll kill her," he muttered to himself.

He called Shortie again. "Shortie, this Joy woman is giving me nothing but trouble!"

"So she's smarter than you thought," Shortie observed with a laugh.

"It doesn't matter. I'm going to win. But she's reported me to the DMV. I have to take my driver's license test all over again like a teenager!"

"Ha! Really? That's rich. How'd she think of that? She must be a *creative* artist!"

"Too creative! She's trouble. I still haven't gotten my money. The bills are piling up! It's been a whole month. I can't believe she can stall things like this. I feel like killing her!"

"Well, don't resort to anything that drastic. Accident-staging is one thing. Murder is another. You'll probably still get your money."

"But when? When! I sure picked the wrong victim. She didn't look all that smart. Now I'm matching wits with her. I explained to Hopeford several times. She came out of the post-office without looking."

"Let the games begin! Score one for her!" Shortie laughed again.

"Hey, you just gave me an idea. I can give her trouble with the DMV too!"

"How so?"

"I can have Mel Grant write a letter saying she hasn't got any liability insurance. They'll cancel her driver's license! Ha! I'll get even with her. She won't be going anywhere!"

"Great idea. Let me know what happens!"

"Bye for now."

The next week at the DMV, tall forty-two-year-old Gaude Velasquez found himself standing in a line of twenty sixteen-year olds waiting to take their driver's license test. He had arrived right after lunch at exactly one p.m.

"This is humiliating," he muttered under his breath. Velasquez watched one chewing bubble gum, blowing fat bubbles in front of his mouth which would then collapse all over his face. Another was picking his nose, rubbing boogers on his shirt. A thin, short boy played with his yo-yo, while a girl next to him in a plaid dress with a white collar braided her long, dishwater-blonde hair while yawning in boredom.

Gus looked at his watch. Two o'clock and still he found himself at the end of the line of all these first-time drivers. An hour wasted in waiting. His anger flared. He was a spectacularly good driver, who, like a hunter, aimed and struck at precisely the right moment. That took skill. That took wits and daring, courage and experience. He was a superb driver. The best! He had to be good to earn his money.

Finally, after waiting forever, at 4 p.m. the instructor called his name. When he saw Gaude, he let out a loud gawfa. "Sorry, about that," the instructor apologized. "I've been working with teeny-boppers all afternoon. Are you here to renew your license?"

"I was informed I had to take the test over. I don't know exactly why," Gaude evaded. "Maybe it was a mistake."

"Well, you're here. So let's go."

Gaude slipped behind the wheel while the instructor got into the passenger seat of the fairly new dull-gray Ford they provided for him. He had told them his car was in the shop. He turned the key to start the engine and headed for the street. Gus reined in an impulse to hit a fire hydrant and get his life over with. He felt so ridiculous. He would definitely get even with this Joy woman. Who did she think she was putting him in this ridiculously awkward position? Wasting his precious time when he could be out on the road earning money. Did the instructor know his secret? He hadn't said anything. Did Joy go around telling everyone that he was a criminal? He would get her. He would provoke her anger and frustration, just like he felt now.

"You did a fine job," the instructor said after Velasquez had gone around the block, parallel parked, and gone out on the freeway past a few exits, before returning to the plain, dull cinderblock DMV building

"You passed. Just remember to respect other drivers."

"Oh, definitely," Guade agreed. His face turned red with anger. He would get her for this. She would pay in spades!

The next day he reminded Mel to write a letter to the DMV.

Chapter Eleven

Arriving home after an exhausting day at the studio, Joy opened her mailbox. She had just swept and mopped the entire studio after a long day of painting. Joy had cleaned the bathroom and reorganized the top of her paper drawers, dusting and rearranging the photographs she had of her showings. It was a relief to be home. She would feed Brandy, who was standing excitedly next to the door in anticipation, make dinner for herself, fix her brown-bag lunch for tomorrow, and chop fruit for her morning smoothie.

The mail revealed a strange letter from the DMV. She read it over three times trying to make sense of it.

"YOUR DRIVER'S LICENSE IS CANCELED. DO NOT DRIVE. YOUR DRIVING PRIVILEGES ARE SUSPENDED."

The letter went on to explain that because she did not have any liability insurance, she would be unable to drive anywhere anymore.

"What?" she exclaimed out loud in disbelief. Didn't they know that she had Hopeford Insurance which she had carried for twenty-seven years without interruption? Didn't they have that information on their computers? Joy was stunned.

She called Carey. "Would you believe the DMV has cancelled my driver's license!"

"Why?"

"They say I don't carry liability insurance!"

"Didn't they check? I would be angry. Call them tomorrow and straighten them out immediately. They probably got this 'information' from that Velasquez guy or his lawyer, then sent the letter without checking first. Completely idiotic and inefficient. You can clear that up very easily. You have a copy of your insurance information, don't you? I always carry mine in the glove compartment."

"Oh, yes. I have two copies."

"So that's simple. Just send that to them. Just another bureaucracy error. Someone too lazy to look it up. The department shouldn't just send you a letter suspending your driving privileges without first checking. Anyone can tell them you don't have insurance. Would they believe anyone? I'd call them also."

"Thanks. I'll do that first thing."

So he was trying to get even. Didn't he do enough damage? Joy's ankle still hurt at times, especially in rainy weather. She felt bruised in more ways than physical. And why did she have to fight with Hopeford? She paid them regularly! For twenty-seven years. Yet they seemed to be taking Velasquez's side. She felt a dark tug-of-war with him. A complete stranger, he had sideswiped into her life and created turmoil that went on and on like a dark maze she couldn't find her way out of. Her mail seemed to always have terrible news: Hopeford's accusations, threats from the DMV, who knows what next?

Didn't she have enough problems and frustrations in her life, trying to continue being an artist in a slow economy and without any gallery representation for the first time in her life? The Museum's Artist's Gallery had always come through with a check whenever she was on the brink of disaster financially. Now they wanted to send the last two drawings back. However, they kept renting and being renewed.

Eventually, they would send them back.

Joy had lots of new work to send out. But where? Her former dealer in San Francisco used to call with urgency."We badly need new work." She would send paintings and drawings and soon would have checks. Bravitski always had a show somewhere in L.A. and once in a while in New York too. She had been in group shows in Chicago and Philadelphia and even once in Germany. Now there wasn't even one show on the horizon. Nowhere to go, nowhere to show. Life at the studio continued as always, while the work stacked up. She no longer had enough space to stack it all.

Her auto insurance would go up. It was just business as usual for Hopeford. They didn't want an expensive lawsuit. It was easier and more profitable to just raise her rates. They didn't care that they were aiding and rewarding a criminal. If they paid him, they would just feel relieved to get rid of the case. And she couldn't just cancel her insurance. It was the law. She had to have auto insurance.

Everyone had to have auto insurance. And soon everyone might have to have health insurance too. Health insurance was even more of a fraud, Joy believed. She had never had it until Medicare kicked in. Now she didn't use it. Going to the Y, making her smoothies, eating her carrots just like Brandy did everyday, and going to the spa kept her fit and healthy. She never caught a cold or the flu.

Health insurance was for people who did not take care of themselves and who did not believe in their own power to heal themselves. She shunned prescription drugs also. So called "medications" made a lot of money for pharmaceutical companies while killing people with their "side effects." She believed so-called "side-effects" were effects. There was no such thing as "targeted therapy" with drugs. They went everywhere and did damage throughout the body. Yet people took pills because it was easier than changing their lives. It was easier to pop a pill than adopt a regular exercise schedule and give up sweets and fat-laden, greasy food.

As for surgery, Joy believed cutting into the body was the wrong thing to do. Maybe if she was shot, the bullet would have to be dug out. This was not a far-fetched scenario in Los Angeles. Highland Park, where she worked, was full of gang violence and graffiti artists. Gunfire was a threat everywhere in L A. now.

A truck would come by once a week to clean her studio windows of spray- painted "Art." Graffiti was the least threatening crime. Other crimes might be injurious and require medical attention. The area was not safe. But any area in Los Angeles was dangerous at times.

And if Joy broke bones, she would need a cast. But still the body would have to heal the bones back together. The cast would just hold the limb stiff. Joy had very strong bones. She had never broken any of them despite accidents and falls. She would never take drugs to attempt to prevent bone loss. Weight-lifting and walking kept them strong. Joy felt her bones were like iron after she lifted the barbells at the Y. She felt very strong. Yet Joy knew the fragility of the body when over- challenged, for instance when faced with an opponent such as a gun or an automobile.

She called the DMV. "Just send a copy of your insurance, the slip they have you carry in your car. You can still drive. We might have sent that letter out without checking first if an attorney complained."

Joy tried not to live in fear. She could still drive. She could still walk, for God's sake! She chanted morning and evening in front of her Gohonzon for protection. Chanting was a form of prayer. The Buddhists believed that chanting provided protection from the Gods. Being "in rhythm of the Universe" because one chanted provided good fortune or "luck." Joy felt lucky that she had gone through many close calls and still was healthy and functioning very well into her sixties. One of her "near-death" experiences was being run into as a pedestrian. She had been crossing Old York on the green light across the street from her studio about fifteen years ago. A left-turner had failed to stop.

Her thought, as the split-second arrived before the car hit her, "My life is over. I've had a good life. This is the end."

She had been hit hard, the car smashing against her leg, and hoisted into the air like a balloon bloated with helium. Joy fell down so hard on the black, gravel road, she had thought she'd made a hole in it. Instead, astounded that she was still alive, Joy had gotten up and limped to the sidewalk. She had made it back to the studio, a short walk that seemed miles. Calling her doctor and an accident attorney, she began a ten-year journey of pain. However, she still walked, she still worked throughout that painful time. The attorney had sent her to various doctors and physical therapists.

One of the first doctors she had gone to had put her in a room covered in plaster dust. He had come in and palpitated her leg but could find nothing amiss. Her leg, though aching with soft-tissue injury and damage, besides being black and blue, had not sustained further harm.

"They always break bones," the doctor had marveled at her straight leg.

"I did a couple of years of aerobic dance at the old Jack LaLanne gym," she had told him. Joy remembered going to the old gym in Burbank where high-impact aerobic dance exercises were held for half an hour. She had gotten good enough to teach, and led once when the instructor failed to show. Her friend, Fay, was better than she was. Her stamina amazed Joy. She always tried to keep up with Fay, an impossibility. However, her bones became iron rods supporting her.

"Your time has not come to die," Carey had remarked back then. "You still have much to accomplish."

"Yes, I guess you're right. By all odds, I should have died or become a cripple. But somehow, I came through without permanent damage. I can stand pain. It's a part of living. I'm alive, that is the main thing."

The lawyer had managed to get her nine thousand dollars after he took his share. Almost one thousand a year for ten years of searing pain.

Old York was treacherous. It looked like an ordinary street. But it was full of crazies.

She had just met another one.

Chapter Twelve

"I thought you were getting a check from Hopeford," Maria complained. "It's been over a month."

"Yeah, I thought so too," Gaude agreed. "I don't know what's holding it up."

"We have those bills, just stacks. They need paid. And we really need a new heater for the house. Winter is just around the corner. You know ours leaks gas. It should have been replaced last year. It's not safe to turn it on."

"I'm sure we will get that check soon. We should have gotten it already."

"Juanita and Jorge are going to need school clothes soon. It's already almost September. We need to go shopping at the mall. Pants, dresses, socks, shoes, all of it."

"I know. I'll see what I can do to hasten it along." Gaude loosened the top button of his shirt that had suddenly become too tight, choking him. He was beginning to feel dubious about ever getting paid. It had seemed like such a sure thing. His aim had been spectacular, his timing superb. He had prided himself on a job well-done. He was getting angrier by the day at this Joy lady. She couldn't be so smart as to figure it out, could she? He had gotten her to apologize. The more he thought about it, the more he wanted to follow her.

He needed to figure out her game. She needed to be eliminated. She must be the blockade that was keeping him in debt. He had his lawyer, the letters had been written. Yet it was over a month. He hated to go out to do another job right now. He still had pain and injuries. His kids were still sore and stiff. No, he couldn't do another job for a while. He had been counting on the money from Hopeford.

Gus's anger increased at this Joy lady he had the misfortune to select. Who was she, anyway? His curiosity was piqued. He needed to find out a bit about her, snoop and spy a bit. So he could scare the heck out of her.

Yes, that was he needed to do. He would begin a campaign, not stalking per se, but close. He would get even. She was blocking his progress. This incident should have been so easy. He had planned it right, hit her perfectly, his split-second judgments had been accurate, right on target. He had followed it up with intimidation. He had smooth-talked her into a confession; at least that bitch had said she was sorry.

The neighborhood was a low-rent area. If she was so smart, what was she doing in that run-down part of town? She must be vulnerable. He needed to find her sore spot and hit the right buttons to make her stop her resistance. Whatever she was telling or writing Hopeford was convincing them to withhold his check. He would get her to STOP. He must begin tomorrow. Velasquez knew her phone number, her address, her private information. It should be easy. Just go on a scare campaign. He would get her frightened enough to stop her tactics. He would begin tomorrow. How about if he started right now?

He picked up the phone.

Joy was ready to close the studio when the telephone rang. It was nearly five o'clock and the light had faded into near blackness. She did not like to stay much after five. The area was full of gang violence. She often heard gunshots piercing the night air. One of those nights her windows had been shattered. She had come into the studio to work, only to be shocked to find shattered glass covering the office floor and a large hole in the window. A brick lay in her office surrounded by the glass shards. That morning had been spent, not painting and drawing as she had planned, but sweeping glass and calling the window replacement companies in the area. She then had to wait for them to arrive with the plate glass that once more would protect her paintings. The replacement took more than an hour. Another day shot to Hell by hotshots!

Joy picked up the phone. Silence. *"Hello, who is this?"* she demanded, before realizing it was a silent call. She slammed the phone down. Who was calling her? Who was trying to intimidate her? The police would ask if she had any enemies, Joy knew from once when she had received a string of silent calls. They had warned her that stalking often led to murder. Bravitski hadn't any enemies that she knew of. It was probably a prank caller. Nothing had happened to her then. But that was then, now was now.

Now… her thoughts flashed upon Gaude Velasquez. She had successfully gotten a police report. Her constant stream of letters and phone calls had worked to stall Hopeford from writing that creep a check. Even the police report *number* had worked temporarily. Joy still did not have the actual report. But Hopeford had decided to send a detective to her studio. He had contacted her but had been too busy, as yet, to come over to interview her. Joy wondered if she should inform the police. But she wasn't sure this call was from Velasquez. How could she know? She had caller I.D. on her home telephone only. It could have been anyone.

Joy shrugged her shoulders and closed the garage door as she went out. *She must not show fear.* The Buddhist Gods protected her when she chanted. She must be strong. Yet her fear rose to the surface as Joy was reminded of the invisible tug-of-war she was having with Velasquez. Gaude must be furious. He certainly was a good shot, using his junk car as his weapon. He had aimed it perfectly. He had seemed to read her mind, crossing over into her lane just as the thought came to her that she must get away from "this weirdo." He must be very practiced at this sort of horrendous crime. She shuddered.

This man *was* a dangerous character. And she lived and worked alone. But she was strong! Yet Joy couldn't help wishing that she had stopped in front of the mailboxes instead of going into that small parking lot. Avoiding meeting Velasquez would have been far superior to this dark, zigzag war she was waging. If that phone call had been him, he was stalking her. Drawing that conclusion out meant he might attempt to kill her, get her out of his way, so he could collect the insurance money. She wondered just how desperate he was. Taking his children with him probably indicated *extreme* desperation.

She probably should call the police.

Instead when she got home and had fed Brandy, she called her friend Carey.

"Do you think that Velasquez guy would stalk me?"

"Why do you think he would do that?" Carey asked.

"He isn't getting any money and it's been over a month. He must be angry. He was arrogant enough to believe I couldn't see through his scheme."

"You may be right. Be careful. Has anything out-of-the-ordinary occurred?

"I got a silent call just as I was leaving the studio. It gave me a weird feeling. It may have been him."

"You might get caller I.D. on the studio phone. You said you have it at home."

"That's a good idea, though it isn't one hundred percent. Many calls just say 'private call' or 'unknown.'"

"Probably a waste of money. Though it might be good to have it."

"I'll call the phone company tomorrow and order the service."

"By the way, Stan wanted to go to the Hollywood Bowl on Saturday night. Joni Mitchell is singing from her new album as well as some of her old hits. Would you like to join us?"

"Yes, for sure! Love her CDs. She's an original."

"Stan asked if you would pick up the Joni Mitchell tickets he ordered. They're at Will Call."

"I could go on Friday night on my way to my film developer."

"Great! They're open until ten at night."

"I'm looking forward to hearing the parking lot song! You know, 'They paved paradise to put up a parking lot...'" Joy sang. "And I can see the lot from *Both Sides Now*." She laughed. "Excuse me, that's Judy Collins! Just a little mix-up."

Carey laughed. "Joni sings it too! You aren't completely mixed up! We'll enjoy all versions of everything that she sings. Got to go. I've got Lasagna in the oven ready to come out."

"Sounds delicious. Bye."

The next day Joy finished up a roll of film, shooting her crayon drawings. She cleaned up the studio, sweeping and mopping, then closed up. The Hollywood Bowl was less than a half-hour away. The reliable truck started right up and she was soon passing the rolling green hills of Hollywood. Joy passed the green acres of Forest Lawn Memorial Park where some of her friends who had died too young of Cancer were buried. Joy always said "Hello" as she passed, talking to them, telling them the news. And she always told them she loved them. "May your spirit dwell in peace," Joy called, waving as she glided past. The sadness she felt was an extra weight she carried that driving onward didn't help.

The Hollywood Freeway was jammed as usual, but Joy took Barham running alongside it. She wondered where to park. There was a lot across the street that connected to the Bowl with an underground tunnel. This was easy; she had done it before. That choice was familiar. The tunnel was long, but they kept it fairly clean. Here and there you could see evidence of bums having taken up residence at one time or another. Graffiti adorned the walls. Some urine spots could not be scrubbed out. She decided to park in that lot and walk the tunnel anyway.

Arriving at the large parking area, Joy found it fairly empty. A few cars here and there made for a sparse-looking lot. She thought of Joni Mitchell's song and laughed aloud. She parked, locked up her truck and jumped out.

She found the tunnel easily enough. But it was already getting dark. Days were already getting shorter and the light got dimmer much earlier. She looked at the tunnel dubiously. Perhaps it wasn't safe at this hour on a deserted night. It was almost six. It would be different if there was a crowd. But the tunnel looked empty. Joy had taken this tunnel many times. But she had never taken it alone. "It's perfectly safe," she muttered, trying to convince herself.

Joy entered the tunnel. The music in her head changed from Joni Mitchell's *Big Yellow Taxi* to Franz Schubert's Eighth (Unfinished) Symphony, dramatic music that seemed to reverberate in the empty tunnel. She supposed the symphony had remained unfinished because Schubert's life had been cut short. He died when he was only about thirty-one. Joy wondered what had happened to him, and as she began walking the dark tunnel, she vowed to look up his biography. She could Google him on the Internet. Such a waste of talent! He could have composed many more striking melodies had he lived out his lifespan. She wondered what killed him at such a young age. Perhaps he had enemies.

Joy suddenly thought she heard footsteps behind her. A tap-tap-tap became progressively louder as if a person were following her. She dreaded looking behind her, but quickly did. In the blackness, she saw nothing.

Nevertheless, she quickened her steps. Joy supposed she could run, but she was feeling bit fatigued from her long day of painting, taking photos, and cleaning the studio. She walked faster. Another furtive glance back revealed a shape behind her and a glint of steel. Someone was coming after her with a knife! Could this be her overactive imagination? She thought of Schubert and broke into a run. Someone in back of her repeated her movement and was running also.

She could now see the end of the tunnel. "I see the light at the end of the tunnel," she laughed, amusing herself. She tried to quash the panic that was beginning to build inside of her. Her nerves were raw with fear. Her heart thudded loudly in her chest. *Yes, she did have an enemy now.* Someone, Velasquez, was extremely angry at her. Was that him behind her? Her heart began to ache and she felt a stitch in her side.

Joy quickly glanced once more behind her but the tunnel only revealed an amorphous shape in its blackness. There definitely was someone behind her with a knife, running in her direction. She broke into a fierce gallop with all the strength and wind she had left.

Finally, she reached the end of the tunnel. There were people scattered around. Joy breathed a sigh of relief as she made her way up the hill to the ticket booths.

"Will Call for Stan Moshan," Joy stated to the ticket seller, a plump woman with a generous, pleasant face. The woman glanced at her lists.

"Yes, we have them," she reported, smiling as she pulled the tickets out from her files. "You will really enjoy Joni. She's not only a genuine original, her voice is angelic and she's gorgeous!"

"Yes, I wouldn't want to miss it," Joy uttered breathlessly. She had almost whispered. She was winded from her ordeal. Her hands shook from the threat she had endured. Was it Velasquez or her over-fried imagination? Was that a knife glinting in the darkness or a key chain, belt buckle or badge? Joy wondered, though she didn't really want to know.

She put the tickets in her purse. Joy decided to skip the tunnel on the way back. She would run across the wide streets. It wasn't very busy now. It was almost seven and the streets had cleared somewhat. People were having dinner. Once more, she obliterated from her mind any danger.

Joy approached the streets. She would just play dodge-car like she used to play dodge-ball as a child. Near the Bowl, the south-bound lanes of Highland Avenue, though wide, were not congested. She waited until it was clear and ran across as if her life depended on it. Certainly, it did.

The north- bound side was busier. But the cars had lights. She would wait it out until it was empty, completely dark. This took several minutes. Finally, the road cleared and she quickly ran across safely. Joy giggled nervously, out of breath. Her truck was still where she had parked it. No one was around. She successfully made it to her truck, beeped her electronic door-opener and hopped in. The doors locked automatically after she slammed the door shut. Joy started the truck and the lights automatically lit up the dark area.

Glancing over to her left, she saw a beat-up, dirty white Mercedes starting to leave. The driver was thin, though she couldn't make out any other details. She shuddered. Was that her enemy, Velasquez? It looked like him. It was the same type of beat-up Mercedes. Oh God! Had he come after her with a knife? Was her life about to end too early, though not as early as poor Schubert, who created such magnificent music? Joy trembled at the thought. Perhaps she had just experienced a close-call with death.

Yes, life was precarious. How had she gotten involved with this sleazy character? She had just been driving carefully, slowly straight ahead, minding her own business. Yet now she was in a struggle for the truth, even for her life. She had met up with a criminal and he had entered her life with his anger and his desperation. She was blocking his path to the reward he had planned, even counted on. Now he was after her.

As Joy drove home, she knew she would have the courage to pursue her stand with Hopeford. She would not let Velasquez frighten her into submission.

She would continue trying to convince Hopeford of the truth, even as her life was on the line.

Chapter Thirteen

Detective Stuart from Hopeford Insurance Company sat across from her at the studio. He was a heavyset but short man with nothing to recommend him physically except an interesting black-and-white print shirt that looked crisply new. "I'm going to tape this conversation," the Detective said as he took out his portable device. He set the buttons and began his questions.

"This is Detective Stuart on September 1, 2010. I'm speaking with Joy Bravitsky at 4000 Old York Boulevard in Los Angeles, California at ten a.m. concerning claim 4968. Do you intend to tell the truth?"

"Yes. I swear to tell the truth."

"Exactly what happened on July 13th, 2010, on Old York Boulevard?"

"I was driving straight, having come out of the post-office near Avenue 51. There was a big truck parked in front of the mailboxes that I had to get around. It was difficult to see around it, so I waited until the road was perfectly clear. I cleared the truck and was just breathing a sigh of relief when something made me turn my head to the left.

"It was an energy I felt, almost palpable, next to me on my driver's side. There was a man driving the wrong way, in the wrong lane. He was staring at me like a race-car driver would size up his competition. I thought, 'What is this weirdo doing? I'd better get away from him fast!' As soon as I had that thought, he pulled over into my lane and clipped me with his back-end."

"What did you do then?"

"I pulled over. He had two kids in his car, a toddler and a little girl. He didn't care about them or me. *He didn't act like he was in an accident.* He wanted my insurance information, my driver's license, and my registration. He whipped out his camera and started taking pictures. I was appalled by his efficiency. My thought was that he had done this type of thing before." Joy squirmed in her seat.

"So he was in the wrong lane, driving the wrong direction?" Detective Stuart glanced at Joy in alarm.

"Yes, it's a two-lane road."

"What did you think happened?"

"At first I thought he tried to pass me and didn't have room. People don't like to get behind my truck and often try to pass. But no one has hit me until now."

"So what happened to your vehicles?" Detective Stuart took up his pen.

"I had minor damage to my bumper that I fixed with black oil paint. But he had a dent and a busted tail-light on his passenger side. I noted that he already had a dent in the same spot further up, obviously made some time ago."

"Were you hurt?" Detective Stuart scratched his head with worry.

"I had some soft-tissue injury and saw a chiropractor. My knee had a sharp pain when I climbed the stairs."

"Do you still have pain?"

"No, I swim. I only visited the doctor once. Sometimes, especially when it rains, I still feel it, however."

"Do you think he was hurt?"

"He probably had some soft-tissue injury also. His kids suffered also. He told Hopeford he had three children with him. But there was only two—unless one was in the trunk!"

Detective Stuart didn't laugh at her joke. He was busy fumbling around with his tape recorder. He dealt with the criminal element everyday, so his sense of humor was dulled. He turned off his device and turned to her matter-of-factly.

"Thank you. That concludes this interview." His face was serious, all business.

He turned to Joy and spoke confidentially. "This is off the record but it doesn't look good for you. Even with a police report, there isn't a witness. He's claiming that he had the right-of-way. Unless there's witness, we can't prove he deliberately hit you. *Even if he did.* I'll try to find out more about this character. But I can't promise anything. I'm sorry."

"Can you tell me about accident-staging?" Joy was disappointed but still curious.

"There isn't much to tell. However, I'll tell you one thing. They don't usually bring their kids. This is not a nice man."

The Detective got up to leave. She let him out of the gate and watched him head for his car.

After Detective Stuart had gone, Joy tried to get back to work. Her state of mind was in a frantic jumble. How could she prove she'd been victimized? *No one believed her!* Turmoil often motivated the work. But now she was tangled into a web of frustration and anger.

Joy overcame the paralysis she felt by going through the motions, setting up her drawing paper on her Masonite board, delineating the margins.

"I've got to get back to work," she firmly told herself. Joy took up a fat oil crayon and began slashing the paper. Soon she was engrossed in her drawing. The lines became a tangle of energy. How they transmitted her emotions to an astute viewer seemed to be magic. The tangles had to coalesce into a composition. Raw emotion wasn't sufficient. The drawing had to work. That was where the art came into play. The lines had to evolve into an harmonious whole. There had to be continuity and rhythm to her fury. After a while, she sat back to observe. She was finally calm enough to view her results. Now Joy could see what had to be done. A few more lines here and there and she had made an expressive composition.

She had taken her raw anger and made it coalesce into a statement on the page. This was the transformational power of creativity. Out of dark emotions came beauty.

Thank God she had her art. What would she ever do with her feelings without it?

Chapter Fourteen

Gus was drinking coffee with Shortie in a secluded corner of the Brick Coffee-House. He was extremely angry, exhausted, frustrated. "It's been over three months! I've not gotten a penny from that broad!"

"She's got guts. She must be writing a lot of letters!"

"I'm going to kill her! This should have been so easy! My timing and execution were perfect! She thought I should have slowed down! I fooled her completely."

"But she must have wised up! She must have figured it out."

Gus pounded the table. "I'll get her!" His eyes bulged out and drops of cold perspiration broke out on his rigid, ashen-white face. His face looked haunted, like a vengeful ghost.

As if to stoke his anger, Gus's cell phone rang ominously. "Let me take this," he said to Shortie, cupping his phone with his left hand.

"Hello, Mel. What's the news? She has what! A police... report of some sort? There wasn't a police car in sight, I swear. She what? She went to the police later, just last week? I can't believe it. The police gave

her a detective! Hopeford also gave her a detective! Two detectives!! Damn it to Hell!

"She'll never prove anything! No one saw anything! The one witness was in his shop and came out after the screech! I talked to him and convinced him that she hit me as she came out of the post-office and blocked my right-of-way. I convinced Hopeford that *she* hit me! I can't believe Bravitski went to the police! She was the perfect victim—just a skinny, old hag! Damn the stupid bitch! I'll show her!"

He snapped the phone shut angrily. His hand was shaking and Gus looked like he had just seen a lynch mob coming after him.

Shortie tried to keep a straight face. During the cell-phone conversation, he had found himself rooting for the artist. This confused and disconcerted him.

Trying to calm Gaude down, Shortie changed the subject. "Tell me about insurance. You're so well informed. You know all the ins and outs."

"Damn it!" Gus hesitated and then, as if he were catching his breath, launched into his story.

"I studied to be an attorney, you know." Gus was struggling to gain control of himself, tugging to loosen the buttons of his shirt near his neck. "I only made it for just short of two years. I was a fair student admittedly, nothing to crow about. Then I met Maria; fell in love. She became pregnant with Jorge. I had to quit law school and get a job full-time." He shook his head as if throwing off his rage.

"That's how you know so much about how the law works?" Shortie was relieved to see that Gus was calming down. He took a sip of his hot coffee after stirring it with a spoon.

"I drove a taxi for a while. But in L.A. everyone has a car. So I drove a truck on the highways. But it took me away from Maria and Jorge for too long. So I studied insurance companies to get an understanding of how they work. You see, all insurance is based on *fear*."

"I agree," Shortie nodded. "You're afraid your home will incinerate so you get home insurance. You pay every payment on time. But when you have a claim, they tell you it's tough luck.

Your problem isn't covered. After we had all that rain, my retaining wall fell in two places. I called; made a claim. They told me it was a 'maintenance problem' and refused to pay. They told me it was soil erosion and an old wall. They've eliminated flood insurance, they told me. It is no longer covered under your policy."

"You need a lawyer to get anything out of them these days. All they care about is 'cost-effectiveness' and their 'bottom-line.' It's all profit so they can pay their executives millions of dollars in salaries and bonuses. They can get away with this because fear overrides everything. You will still pay your premium because of the fear that you will lose your home."

"You've conquered your fears?"

"Anyone who lets fear control their actions will never get anywhere in this world."

"The world revolves around fear. It's true. Look at War. We're afraid of terrorists, communists, insurgents, anyone who looks different, acts different, or is different," Shortie observed.

"You're right! Look at religion. Jesus Christ died for our sins. You see his fragile body hanging from the cross, his hands bleeding from the nails in his flesh, pounded into the rough boards. You imagine his pain. This is supposed to free you from Sin. Jesus died for our sins. So you can sin and not feel guilty? You're off the hook! Jesus took care of it. Is that what society thinks?"

Shortie could only nod in dismay. He went to church most Sundays with Rosie and his son.

"It's a dramatic display. Jesus on the cross. Does that make people feel better about their sins? They feel safe? Is that what it's about? Making them feel at peace?"

"That's a good point. Why would people feel safe looking at a guy hanging on a cross with nails through his hands?" Shortie asked. He had never looked at his religion from this angle. He had always "believed." He had always prayed to God.

" No, there's no peaceful feeling! People feel fear when they see the illustration. They don't want to be crucified! Guilt and fear. It's what religion makes you feel. Fear and guilt. That's why I don't attend any church."

"So you don't feel guilty after sinning? You don't feel anything after you smash into someone?" Shortie was incredulous. He stared at Gus trying to comprehend his lack of conscience. Someone had told him Gus was a psychopath. He was starting to understand this label. He was starting to agree. He nodded his head while tilting it like a dog trying to understand his master.

"Sin is my profession. Do I feel guilty? No! Guilt is a silly waste of time. I don't have time for regrets. I don't care about my victims. Why should I? Fear is not in my vocabulary."

"Well, I hope you win this one. That 'stupid old hag' you hit is turning out to be more intelligent than you thought." Shortie thought he was trying to warn Gus of something. What? Maybe he was trying to warn himself.

"Yes, she must be pretty smart. At least she *thinks* she is. But she won't win this one! I know insurance. I know it backward and forward. Eventually, they will pay me. And it won't be a pittance, either."

"Well, good—luck. I've got to get home," Shortie said, pushing away from the table. He drank a last sip of coffee and took up the bill to pay the waiter. "Let me know what happens." He left Gus standing at the table, feeling only relief at getting away from him. Gus was too intense sometimes. His arrogance was so over-the-top. Just too much. Whatever Gus was, a psychopath or maybe just crazy, Shortie, at times, couldn't stand him.

Shortie had been an honest man, a laborer for most of his life. He had earned his money through honest sweat, using his hands, his muscles, his strength. He didn't have and couldn't comprehend the criminal mind. Though Gus had taught him his new trade, he was off-putting. The cruelty Gus exuded was something Shortie could not absorb. He would never admit it, but sometimes Gaude scared the Hell out of him!

Shortie had thought of accident- staging only as a temporary way to make a few bucks. Crime was still repulsive to him. He still considered himself to be an honest man.

Breathing a sigh, he walked toward his car. He must get home. He wanted to regain some peace of mind. He needed to hug Rosie. He needed his family and reassurance that everything was fine.

Chapter Fifteen

The ringing of the phone at the studio interrupted a brash swipe of red across the new canvas Joy had begun a week ago. She put the loaded brush down on the freezer-wrap she used for a pallet, and ran to her office.

"Good afternoon," Joy answered hopefully.

"Hello. Is this Joy Bravitsky the artist?"

"Yes, you reached my studio."

"I don't know if you recall but I bought a small painting from you two years ago on the Studio Tour. I'm Louise Fishbach."

"Oh, definitely. I remember the one with the wine-red slash you said simply made the painting. You told me you would only keep it if your husband liked it. But you didn't bring it back."

"Yes," Louise laughed. "That was me."

"I guess your husband liked it."

"Oh, yes, he did. We went to Italy last summer and he really got into the Baroque artists. He's starting to really appreciate art. He loves your painting!"

"I'm really happy. It's always wonderful to have your work appreciated."

"The reason I called is I'm getting a new office at Disney where I practice law. It's got a large, white wall that is crying out for a big painting."

"I can come over with oil on paper studies and photographs. We can see what works for you."

"It has to come within my budget."

"How much is that?"

"Well, one thousand dollars."

Joy was a little disappointed at that amount. Her budget would only cover a small oil on paper. The old price was twelve-hundred-and-fifty dollars. Her last show had seen the price go up to twenty-five hundred for a three-foot drawing. Louise was conservative. But perhaps she could stretch that budget a bit higher. Joy needed whatever funds she could get right now.

"Let me consult my schedule," Louise said, pausing to check her calendar. "How about next Monday or Tuesday morning between ten and twelve?"

"That would work for me. Can you leave my name at the gate? I have other collectors at Disney. Roy Disney collected my work at his investment office in Toluca Lake. I also have one other collector at Disney so I know you have to be on a list to get through."

"Yes, I will do that. See you next week."

" If it rains, I'll have to postpone. I try not to take Art out in the rain." Although sometimes it did happen she thought, remembering her trip with Chris to Reno. Still it was better not to take unnecessary chances.

"I understand."

"I'll call before I leave the studio."

Joy hung up, jubilant. She loved what was called "in-depth collectors," enthusiasts who wanted more than one work of hers. These collectors were patrons who supported her.

She went back to her canvas full of inspired energy. If she could sell a large work, it would take care of her expenses for several months. That's just what she needed right now. However, Louise had said her budget was only one thousand.

Maybe she could talk Louise into acquiring the larger oil on paper. Joy found just the right one in her paper drawers. It was done in mauves and crimsons, purples and viridian green, the colors Louise would go for. It was around four thousand.

Joy loved selling her own work, being her own "Art consultant." She loved working with collectors, seeing their environment, getting to know a soupcon of their lives. She went again to her paper drawer and began selecting smaller works that she thought Louise might like. She sometimes knew just what to pick based on their personalities and the work that they had been drawn to previously.

Working with galleries was easier sometimes because they dug up the clients. However, Joy usually never got to meet them or see how her Art enhanced their environment. Sometimes she had to fight with galleries to even get the information as to who bought her work, though there was a law on the books in California to that effect, written by Senator Alan Sieroty. She liked to keep a journal book, listing her collectors, what work they bought, when they bought it. Once in a while, the work changed hands so she no longer had the correct information. Or people moved. Some died. Several of her collectors were no longer around to see her shows. This saddened her.

Joy hoped to have a retrospective someday. A retrospective at a Museum! Wouldn't that be wonderful! She wanted so badly to be around to see it, to have a glass of champagne at the opening, watching people react to her work. All her work of different periods: the large spray paintings, the soft-hard-edge paintings, the Rhoplex and acrylic paintings, the *Black Forest* paintings she had done for her grandparents starved to death in the Bergen-Belson Concentration Camp, then the over-size oil crayon drawings she had turned to when her health declined from using the acrylic paint and Rhoplex in big barrels, the fumbling around beginning oil paintings, their evolution into clear glazes, full of saturated color, the oils on paper, and then the tall eight-foot panel drawings. She could fill several museums! Next year, 2011, would mark the fortieth anniversary of creating Art full-time in her studio.

Was this retrospective a dream? Or was this an achievable goal? Joy had almost five hundred collectors amassed over the years.

She had enjoyed so many retrospectives of artists who were no longer alive to clink a champagne glass with her. Rothko had committed suicide in his sixties; Joan Mitchell had drunk herself into ill health, then death, also in her sixties. Joy had visited the Van Gogh Museum in Amsterdam. *She* got to see it; he didn't. He had shot himself in a field, in front of his easel, saying, "What is the use?" Or perhaps, according to a new theory, a teenager shot him. Whatever the facts were, he was only in his thirties when his life ended.

It *was* a tough life. She would never advise anyone to choose art as a profession. Yet Joy knew she would never be able to do anything else. Doing the art was its own reward. She loved to create in the studio all day with only a break for lunch. Without doing Art, she knew her life would be meaningless.

On Monday there was warm sun, much to everyone's relief. Joy had prepared the portfolio of her small oils on paper, wrapping them in plastic just in case. She had a good-looking burlap carry-all with her masking tape, and a new red transparent plastic folder she had purchased for the invoice. She had also splurged on a new outfit in order to be presentable. A forest green pull-over sweater, gray-green denims, and a copper-brown all-weather quilted parka-vest to resist the cold. Everything had been purchased on sale or at a discount. Still, she looked professional and spiffy.

Promptly at 9:30 a.m., Joy called Louise. "Can I take the Golden State Freeway North to get to your office? We lucked out and got sunshine." A good salesperson always presumed there would be no backing out or excuses. She waited anxiously for the reply.

"I never take it. But I suppose you can."

"I already picked several oils on paper. They are ready to put in the truck. I can be at your office within the hour."

"Good. I'll leave your name with the guard downstairs just in case. You can probably find parking on the street. It's not busy today."

"See you soon."

Joy loaded the portfolio of oils on paper into the back of the truck. She felt excited. Her sales were always urgent. There was the usual, never-ending stack of bills in her rack waiting to be paid.

The freeway wasn't too busy. Joy found the exit she needed easily. She had consulted the *Thomas Guide* before she left. It was always better, in Los Angeles, to know exactly where you were going. In the twists and turns, the multiple freeways, the maze of streets, it was oh-so-easy to get totally lost. Too many times her vague idea of where she wanted to go had resulted in confused driving around, wasting time trying in vain to find the right freeway.

Joy arrived promptly and easily found free parking on the street for two hours. But managing two portfolios and her carry-all and over-loaded purse by herself proved impossible. At times like this, she desperately needed Val's help. But Val had gotten a full-time job, she reminded herself. "Here's the efficient Art consultant," she laughed to herself, as she fumbled around, trying to get organized.

Joy dragged the large portfolio forward until she was able to flag a fellow going into the building with a badge clipped onto his jacket. He was willing to help until she got to the guard stand where there was another helper standing by. They went up to the 25th floor in the elevator.

Louise was happy to see her. A very nice lady who would be easy to work with, Joy predicted.

And she was right. Louise was soon enmeshed in looking, trying out, making a decision. After narrowing it down to three oils, she called another attorney into the office for her opinion.

Kathy agreed with Louise's first choice, a purplish out-of-phase landscape-like abstraction. Joy had picked the wall next to Louise's desk for it and the oil on paper sang there, its colors blending and contrasting with the panoramic landscape view of the green hills of Forest Lawn Memorial Park that could be seen through the window. There was an interesting interplay between the real landscape and the imagined oil-on-paper one, as if a dialogue was transpiring. A green place for the dead contrasted with an inanimate abstraction of the living.

Joy wrote up the selection. The price was $1250.

Louise protested mildly, reminding Joy of her budget. Joy responded by coming down to $1200. She would let Louise pay for the frame.

Looking at the oil convinced Louise to agree. She wrote a check.

Joy called her framer, using Louise's phone with her permission.

"I'll be here until three today," Tom said.

"I'll be over in less than an hour," Joy told him. It was eleven-thirty.

"Isn't it hard to sell your work?" Louise asked after Joy had hung up the phone.

"No, the work sells itself."

"I mean, isn't it hard to part with it?"

"No. I'm just the artist."

Louise smiled. Somehow, she got it. Joy was like a parent to her work. A parent raised the child, then let her go to lead her own life.

Louise recommended another attorney, a big collector, who might be interested in Joy's work. She even e-mailed the attorney for her.

Joy was jubilant. The sale was easy. Louise was a very nice lady, just as she predicted, who couldn't resist her paintings. Joy would go to her framer who was near the beach and take the rest of the afternoon off. A little reward for her hard work was in order.

Once Joy was back on the freeway, the sun shone and all seemed glorious. It was the perfect day to visit the ocean, perhaps have lunch at a sidewalk café, and walk alongside the sea. It had rained seven days straight and the sun was a welcome treasure. She felt relieved. The check would clean out her bill rack, even if there would be hardly anything left for savings. She felt relief, as if a big burden had been taken off her shoulders.

Tom was at his frame shop, ready to receive the work. Though his Quonset-hut building was unimpressive, he was the best framer in town. "Louise said to bill her directly. I used to include the frame in the price but these days I just can't afford to do it."

"I'll bill her as I usually do with my other clients," he said. Tom was always nice. She enjoyed working with him. He came without the bloated ego so many had in the art world.

Driving to the short distance to the ocean, Joy spotted a sushi restaurant. "I should have brought my lunch," she chided herself. She had packed a lunch but in her haste had left it at the studio. Sometimes, she brought her bagged sandwich, spread her quilt out, eating at the beach. In California you could do that even in the dead of winter. While her friends back east shoveled snow, Joy would work on her tan.

Today she ate the sushi with relish. The tuna was delicious and she loved the sharp bite of the green wasabi. Miso soup always calmed her down. Japanese food was light, non-fattening. She always felt refreshed after eating it. Joy even splurged on two scoops of green-tea ice cream. After all she had been through, she deserved a treat.

After lunch, she took a walk alongside the ocean, in the park above it. People were happy to see the warming sun and were out strolling. Some brought their cute dogs with colorful knitted sweaters, straining at their leashes. Others brought their delightful children. Smiling and laughing, couples walked hand-in-hand. Joy felt her spirit soar.

Joy pushed her doubts and fears into her subconscious as she viewed the glistening sea. She would forget her troubles for a while. She would not dwell on her failing art career, her lack of galleries, her fall from the pinnacle in the Art World, the outsider role she had fallen into, full of rejections and humiliations.

She would blank out Gaude Velasquez's staring at her, his smooth-talking meanness, his desperation, his cruelty to his children, the black pall he had cast upon her life. His anger and stalking behavior would vanish in the breeze.

Joy would walk in the sunshine feeling the warmth upon her skin, breathe in the salty sea air, so fresh and clean, and enjoy people-watching, walking among the strollers. A bright, sunny day by the ocean could compensate for a lot of darkness in life. The sun would obliterate her troubles, at least for one afternoon.

On a day like this, it was so good to be alive!

Chapter Sixteen

"**O**h my God! Oh, Jesus! Mother of God! What have I done? What ever have I done?"

Shortie was sobbing over the phone. His sobs came in uncontrollable spurts as he tried to catch his breath between convulsions.

"Control yourself, Shortie. What happened? Do you want to come over?" Gus couldn't fathom what was wrong.

"Oh, God! *Someone was killed!*"

"What? Whatever happened? I'll meet you right away at the coffee-shop. Calm down!"

"Yeah, the coffee-shop. I can be there in ten minutes."

Gus dropped his greasy rag. He had been working on the engine of another Mercedes he had found at a car auction downtown. This one was even older, 1980, a piss-green color and cost him all of five-hundred dollars. It blew smoke rings out of its tailpipe, a bad sign. It probably needed new rings, a costly proposition. Now he had new worries.

It sounded as if Shortie was in real trouble. He knew Shortie lacked his skill and split-second timing. But Shortie had been successful in the past. Shortie had bilked a number of insurance companies without much trouble. Had Shortie achieved the worst result? Gus knew full well accident-staging was hazardous. A victim *could* lose control. The whole plan could go awry, blow up in your face. Theoretically, someone could die. Velasquez had never killed anyone. He had been meticulous in his aim, selecting his victim, timing the incident accurately. No one had ever been seriously hurt.

Shortie arrived at the coffee-shop visibly shaken. His face was red from crying. He was trembling in violent spasms. His normally smiling brown face was contorted with anguish. He gestured jerk-ily between sobs as they ordered coffee. Anticipating his upset, Gus had found them a secluded table.

"I tried a left-turner," Shortie gasped. He rubbed his wet face with the sleeve of his plaid flannel shirt.

"I told you that maneuver was way too dangerous!" Gus was indignant. Didn't Shortie ever listen to his lectures?

"I know, yeah, but this seemed easy."

"So what happened?"

"I tried..." Shortie gasped and started crying again. He was convulsed with sobs.

"Slow down," Gus instructed. He offered Shortie another napkin.

"I hit a kid making a left-turn, just at the yellow light. He lost control..."

"Left-turn gambits are too risky!"

"He drove into the hamburger joint, Todd's on Old York near Ave. 47."

"So he busted out a window. So what?"

"No! He...He hit a lady eating at the booth. "

"She alright?"

"I just heard on TV she died!" Shortie was sobbing uncontrol-lably. "And her kid is in a coma."

"So... they won't pin it on you. You had the right-of-way."

"I don't think they will come after me. The kid's car was totaled. They said he lost control. I just kept driving. I only got a few dents."

"You got away free and clear. What are you worried about? It's not even being called a hit-and-run."

"A death! A kid in a coma!" Shortie gasped for air between sobs.

"You got away. That's all that matters!"

"I'm quitting this gig. I'm never going to do this ever, ever again."

"What do you mean? No one is accusing you of anything!"

"I'm going back to brick-laying. I'll never forgive myself!"

"Shortie, get hold of yourself! You're fine. You're not in jail. No one is going to impound your car or take away your driver's license."

"Don't you *care?* I killed someone! An innocent lady in her fifties. She'll never get to eat another hamburger."

Gus stifled a laugh. Another greasy hamburger at Todd's was nothing to miss. Just a cheap place to eat. It was not like hitting someone eating at the Ritz-Carlton, for God's sake.

"Look, thinning the population is a benefit to civilization. The kid will come out of the coma. That lady was probably some low-life broad without a life."

"You don't get it, do you?" Shortie was trying to grasp Gus's cold philosophy when it repelled him. "I took one life and seriously damaged another."

"Look, I tried to teach you. You don't listen. Accident-staging is dangerous! The safest maneuver is the side-swipe that I did with that broad I hit. You don't try fancy accidents like left-turners! They turn out badly, for the most part. You just don't have the same control. Aiming is too difficult. Drivers do lose control. Why did you try it?"

"I needed to pay some debts."

"Look, Shortie. Everything will turn out fine. The kid will recover. The lady is gone but probably no one will ever miss her."

"But I killed her!" Shortie was sobbing again.

Gus put a hand on Shortie's arm. "You got away. That's what counts. You learned your lesson. Try the sideswipe next time."

"There will be *no* next-time. I'll find something, anything! I'll put in toilets, rake leaves, walk dogs, wash dirty dishes, anything, anything that needs done."

"Well, it's up to you. It's your life."

Shortie got up, taking the bill for the coffees. "Look, Gus, I'm thankful for the money I made. Most of it was easy and fast. You were a good mentor. You taught me a lot about what to do. Now I've learned what *not* to do. I'm clearing out of accident- staging. It's not for me."

"You have too much conscience. I just see you as being too honest and caring a person. I can erase things from my mind easily. It just comes naturally to me."

"Well, it taught me a lesson. I'm through!" Shortie had regained control of himself. "I just wish I would have quit sooner, before I killed someone."

"You're a coward!" Gus finally found his anger, his indignation. "I'll tell you what I'm going to do! I'll hit that same broad all over again. Maybe even in the same location! After I get my money. Then I'll hit her again!"

Shortie gasped. "Why her?"

"I just want to show her who's boss, who wins."

"Gus, I thought you were smart. That's the dumbest thing I've ever heard!"

"Just watch me collect the money. And then I'll hit her again and make more money. Her big truck will be my giant piggy-bank!"

"I'd say good-luck, but I think you are really pushing it! Pushing it way too far!" Outside the coffee-shop, Shortie almost tripped on a crack in the sidewalk. He caught himself and glanced up at Gus, his face still incredulous.

"Let me decide. I'll show her. I'll kill her. She's not going to hang me up much longer." Gus took another long stride. He looked up at the gray sky, ominous now with hints of rain to come. In the distance, thunder growled.

"Well, I'll say good-bye then, a final good-bye."

"Good luck, Shortie, raking leaves!" Gus sneered as he quickened his pace in the other direction toward his new junk car.

He turned up his collar as the rain began pelting down hard upon him.

"Hey," Shortie called after him after Gaude had walked half a block. "I'd like to keep in contact. I want to know what happens."

"Sure, Shortie, I'll let you know." Gus ducked into his car and started the engine.

Chapter Seventeen

"Hello Carey, I have good news! It's time to celebrate. I just sold an oil on paper."

"Oh, that's great! Who bought it?"

"An attorney who works for Disney. She wanted a second work for her office. She has a small painting at home."

"She got a good one?"

"Oh yes. She has a very good eye."

"Fantastic. Well, I have great news too!"

"What happened?"

"Stan Moshan asked me to marry him!"

"Wow! Really? That is great news! When did *this* happen?"

"We ate dinner on Ocean Avenue, the new Italian place. Afterwards, we had a moonlight walk on the beach. We were star-gazing and out popped the question. Then he got on his knees on the sand! He pleaded with me! Then Stan joked around that he was groveling and bumbling."

"What did you say?"

"Yes, of course. YES!"

"Oh, I'm so happy for you. You have gone with him how many years?"

"Probably ten. I met him in my fifties. He had just gotten a divorce and wasn't ready for anything serious. So I waited it out!"

"You deserve this proposal for your patience."

"Thanks. I knew I couldn't live without him. He just cheers me up and always makes me laugh!"

"So when is the wedding?"

"We haven't picked a date yet. But probably this summer."

"A June wedding?"

"Too trite. We'll probably get hitched in July. Maybe have the wedding at the beach."

"If I can help with the plans, let me know."

"Thanks. Lots to do. When we get the invitations, you can come to a mailing party to help address them."

"How about the dress? I can go with you to pick it out."

"Yes, that would be fun. Let's do that soon."

"Just let me know when you're ready."

"Probably next week. I'll talk to Stan first. He knows you have good taste. He'll trust you to help me select something wonderful."

"I can't wait. Call me when you're ready."

Joy went back to her canvas. It had looked so good when she left it in the evening. But oils changed as they dried. They became flatter. They changed color slightly. Some colors needed another coat. Some areas needed eliminated. She took a wide brush, filled it with saturated color and swiped it across the lower left-hand corner. The magic happened. Many small details were wiped into a cohesive whole. It had just gotten too busy there. The transparent medium she used allowed some of it to show through. Just enough, so the area wasn't flat.

She had been using a lot of dark colors lately, reaching for her tubes of ivory black and indigo. The darkness in her life came out in her art. She could look at her painting and see her mood. She couldn't shake the tumult in her life created by the deliberate "accident." Often she "saw" Gaude staring at her, stalking her, angrily waiting for his payment. A horror movie played repetitiously in her mind's eye. His force, an evil energy, weighed upon her. Joy felt a heaviness, a bleakness in her life she could not shake.

She sat back and gazed at her progress, trying to concentrate on her work.

Painting enthralled her. Other artists might be interested in their careers, getting in with the "in crowd," making a lot of money. But Joy was hooked on painting. She was often oblivious to everything else. When she was transfixed by the strokes and colors on the canvas, board or paper, the whole world disappeared. Her concentration was acute. Sometimes the phone ringing would "wake her up" as if she had been enmeshed in a dream.

Joy stopped at noon to eat her bagged lunch. She always brought the newspaper and library books with her to read a bit. After lunch she took a half-hour nap. Her energy would return after a good rest. That way she could paint and draw until five o'clock. People might refer to her as "prolific." But working every weekday on her Art and sometimes Saturday too, was a necessity to her, just as she must breathe, eat and sleep. Art was as much a part of her life as any basic human necessity. It was hard for others to understand that it wasn't just "work."

When times were hard financially, relatives had helpfully suggested she "do something else." But there wasn't any choice for Joy. She had been born an artist. She would do her art until she dropped dead, the paint brush still clutched in her hand! She would somehow find a way to continue.

Joy had lived at the poverty level for most of her life. She was so used to it she didn't think twice about it. Whatever money she had mostly went back into her Art. She bought her clothes at discount stores and wore old clothes most days to paint in. Her prices had never been very high. The most she had ever received was eleven thousand for an eight-foot painting it had taken many months to create. The collector had made payments. Getting a large sum all at once happened only a few times. When she had dealers, they took fifty percent if they were honest. Often they said they would take fifty percent but when she got the check, she could see plainly they had taken more.

One dealer said he had paid her fifty percent of the agreed price. But when she met the collector by pure chance, he told her he had paid a thousand more! She had confronted the dealer, then left. The art market was unregulated. David Hockney called the art world "ICS," International Crooks and Swindlers.

Yet Joy knew she needed to plug back into the gallery system. Dealers did not understand her new work. Original art was the hardest. It didn't look like anything they had seen before. The easiest route was to do work that looked like Cy Twombly, Picasso, or some already well-known artist. Joy's new work didn't look like anyone else's. Her work looked like Joy Bravitski! Gallery owners would see the photographs of the new paintings, then reject them. It wasn't something they *knew*.

Dealers were a necessary evil because they could give the artist a show. It was only through shows, sales and attention from museum curators that a reputation could be built. Becoming a "name" artist caused the prices to rise, created a demand for the work.

Yet, perversely, this created art as a commodity, a saleable item. Few artists could withstand this pressure and still produce great art, still grow as an artist. It was so easy to get stuck in a style that sold. Because a painting sold, why not do another one in blue? This would mean more money. But this was the pathway to Artist's Hell. Thinking in this vein, this mind-set, violated the tender kernel of art that needed to be protected against "selling out." An artist that fell into the trap of producing for the market often lost the ability to create Art. That was the paradox: the tender trap of success. The art had to keep evolving; the market place stunted its growth.

Every artist in the history of art had faced the same problem. Some were more successful than others at tackling it.

William Turner, who painted in the 1800's, was one of Joy's favorite artists. He had become a member of the official Academy at a young age. He eventually built his own gallery. An illustration in a book about the artist shows a short little man in a tuxedo showing his work to a lady in a long, flowing dress. In addition to his own gallery, he sold his work through dealers and did commissions. He had wealthy collectors and stayed at their castles and mansions. He became rich from his art.

Yet critics attacked him. A cartoon in the book showed a short man with a soaked mop attacking his canvas with "whitewash." Another reviewer criticized his magnificent painting of the *Burning of the Houses of Parliament* because he painted the fire burning in the wrong direction! He was honored and reviled, praised and criticized.

Yet he was able to travel, draw and paint and lived a long, prosperous life.

Joy looked to Turner as a model for her life.

At least she hadn't ever turned to crime. She hadn't used her vehicle to go around crashing into people to collect their insurance! Her horror over Gaude's staged accident never seemed to subside. She was haunted by this dark force in her life. It affected every color she used, every brushstroke she laid down. It affected her nightmarish dreams, her haunted days. Yet she would write still another diatribe to Hopeford. And each time they would promptly write back that it would be another ninety days for them to reach a conclusion. She had succeeded in dragging out their final decision for months. But would Velasquez eventually win? And if he did win, would he try again whenever he ran out of money? This was a far-fetched idea, so ridiculous she shrugged it off.

Still, Joy felt like she was on a precipice looking out over a dark chasm of fear.

Chapter Eighteen

Buddhist meetings were often held in people's homes. Sharon Murphy resided in a beautiful townhouse in upscale Altadena where chanting sessions were often held usually on Sunday morning. The peaceful setting with its shade trees and central courtyard with a small swimming pool was inviting. Sharon also radiated a warmth that embraced visitors to the beautiful condominium she so generously shared with the group. She had grown up in a wealthy family. Her matching crimson denims and bulky-knit cowl-neck sweater attested to her taste in clothes. Her hair was also beautifully cut. Although she now struggled financially, no one would know it from her environment or her personal presentation. She had once had a good job but had been laid off, ironically in the insurance industry. Now she scrambled to make ends meet.

Joy always looked forward to visiting Sharon, and to the meetings where chanting, a form of prayer, was followed by group discussion. Joy had a problem to discuss, one that she had been unable to solve on her own. The darkness she had encountered on the streets of Los Angeles had followed her into the studio. Gaude's cruelty and cunning had made an inroad into her thoughts and feelings. She wanted to know how to win and how to shake off his evil influence. How to turn this "accident stager" into some benefit in her life. Could there possibly be any benefit from a meeting with a criminal?

Changing poison into medicine was a basic Buddhist teaching. She knew that this Velasquez guy had a Buddha nature somewhere within his smooth-talking, cold exterior. There was goodness there, somewhere! But where? She was disgusted with his attempt to rip off her insurance company by harming others. She also believed in karma—cause-and-effect. What effect would his vile actions bring back to him?

"What do you think of a guy who goes around staging accidents to collect insurance money and even takes his kids with him?" Joy asked Sharon shortly after she arrived.

"Buddhism is about cause-and-effect," Sharon reminded her. "We'll talk about this after we chant. Others might have some ideas as to how to deal with this situation."

Soon the group arrived and faced the Gohonzon, a scroll in a cabinet used to chant the Lotus Sutra. The scroll of calligraphy was written in Sanskrit. In front of the cabinet was placed fresh fruit and incense. There was also a metal cup to strike as a bell to begin the prayers. They began by chanting *Nam Moho Renge Kyo* over and over for about twenty minutes. The explanation of the words: Devotion to the mystic law of cause and effect through sound vibration. To elevate one's life condition was a goal. Everyone could also chant for benefits, something they desired. Material things were included as they were thought to lead to enlightenment. You could chant for anything or anyone. When someone was ill, you could chant for their health. When someone caused you pain, you could chant for their happiness.

While Gaude Velasquez had seemed happy with the results he had obtained by smacking into her truck, she knew that he must deep-down be an unhappy soul. No one could obtain happiness by harming others, even if there was a cash reward. She couldn't fathom his state of mind but guessed that attempting to earn money by causing others pain, including his own children, and risking others' lives as well as his own, would only lead to torment. Mentally, he must be a bit sick, she thought. He must be in pain psychologically as well as physically from the "accident."

The group chanted the Lotus Sutra after the resonant gong was sounded. In unison, their voices melded to a powerful force. This achieved getting them in "the rhythm of the Universe." The law of the Universe was "cause and effect." Joy knew this but wondered what karma she had developed to attract this strange, creepy individual into her life.

After chanting, they took their chairs downstairs for the discussion. Joy picked the overstuffed sofa and relaxed into it. She really wanted to get this problem that perplexed and haunted her out into the open. She wanted to know how to handle it from a Buddhist perspective. They might have some advice. Often they just told her to chant about it.

"Are there any guests?" Sharon opened.

Ed raised his hand. His was a tall, blonde surfer type. "I brought Danny," he said. Danny, a dark-skinned skinny young man, must have been retarded because he carried a Teddy Bear with him and sunk strangely, shyly in his chair, hugging the stuffed toy to his chest. No one minded because they knew the transformative practice of Buddhism would help him. "Welcome," Sharon said warmly.

"Let's have an explanation of the practice for Danny," Sharon said.

Lilly got up, a tall, slim brunette. She stood in front of the group confidently.

"Buddhism originated in India. It came down to Japan through Nichirin Dishonan who founded this practice. We chant to the Gohonzon to change our karma, elevate our life-condition, and bring out our Buddha nature both in ourselves and others. We chant morning and evening, doing the *Lotus Sutra* and chanting *Nam Myho Renge Kyo.*

We obtain benefits when we chant both conspicuous and inconspicuous. Chanting gets us in the rhythm of the Universe. We chant for World Peace, a fundamental principal in our practice.

The last prayer is always for our ancestors, that they may live in the spirit world in peace and harmony. Our goal is to achieve enlightenment."

"Thank you, Lilly. Now we will have our discussion. Does anyone want to discuss a problem that involves karma?" Sharon asked.

" I do," Joy volunteered.

"Yes, Joy, you go first. You seem to have something urgent to discuss."

"My truck was hit by an accident stager last July. He had two children in the back seat, a toddler and a little girl. It's almost four months ago, I admit. But I've been fighting with my insurance company ever since. I write letters, call often and went to the police. But even with a police report that explains clearly that I'm not at fault, Hopeford doesn't believe me and sides with him. They seem to want to pay him off which will only encourage his criminal activities, and also raise my insurance rate. He has an attorney which scares them. They don't want to get involved in a law suit. I just don't know what to do to convince them."

"Did you try getting a lawyer?" Sylvia, a thin, earnest red-head asked.

"Yes, I tried Bill @ Bigger Verdict .com, Lou @ Large Payout. com, and Ann @ Award Now.com." Joy joked. She had tried contacting lawyers, but they all had turned her down.

Everyone laughed.

"They don't want to take a case where the victim has a few soft-tissue sprains and strains, only spends fifty dollars for one chiropractor visit, and fixed her scratched rubber bumper herself with shoe polish and oil paint!"

More laughs.

"They want a paraplegic. Someone so deformed that they can make a ton of money!"

"So a lawyer is out. You'll have to resort to chanting," Sharon observed.

"If you chant, you can change your karma," Ed observed. "He will be punished for his 'cause'. He made a destructive cause in the name of greed. Remember that effects are inherent in causes. It's simultaneous, though the concrete results might not show up immediately. He will get that destruction back, whether it's right away or two weeks from now, or two years from now."

"The simultaneity of cause and effect," Sylvia reminded Joy. "Every cause you make contains an effect. It's the Law of the Universe.

"Chant and let the Universe take care of this problem," Sylvia continued. "You don't have to do anything else. You don't even need a lawyer. Earthly justice is nothing compared to Spiritual Justice. The Law of the Universe is irrefutable. He will see the results of his conniving and evil intent. You can count on it."

"I know this is far-fetched, but what do I do if he tries it again after my insurance company pays him off?"

"You are protected by the Universe as long as you chant. You also have to be very watchful."

"As it is, I drive now like a paranoid-schizophrenic!"

More laughter.

Sharon smiled, then closed the conversation. "Thank you Joy for an example of 'cause-and-effect'. Does anyone else have a problem to discuss?"

George raised his hand. "I had car-karma problems too!'

More laughter.

"I was getting way too many tickets. My sports car just wants to go, go, go! But I got tired of Driver's Training courses, paying tickets. I was spending a fortune and wasting a lot of time. So I decided to change my car-karma!"

"What did you do?" Ann piped up. She was a plump but handsome young woman who chanted regularly.

"I began watching my 'causes.'" I watched the speedometer like a hawk, was careful at yellow lights to stop, began looking in my rear-view mirror for police cars!"

More laughter.

"I haven't gotten a ticket in over a year."

Everyone clapped.

"In Buddhism you can change your karma. Even your car karma! It doesn't matter what you have done in the past. It's from this moment on."

"Yes, I've learned that the past isn't something to dwell on, to weigh you down," Ann agreed. "My parents were alcoholics. It was hard for me to relate to people. I found I was afraid and intimidated by anyone who wanted to associate or become friends with me. I decided to change my karma and give people a chance. Not everyone is cruel like that driver who hit Joy's car. There are nice drivers out there who are considerate, who let you in!"

Laughter and nodding from the group.

The discussion went on for an hour. Most of the people were working on changing their karma. At the end of the meeting, they chanted *Sansho,* the *Nam Myoho Renge Kyo* phrase three times to close the meeting and express appreciation and respect to the Gohonzon.

Joy was in a hurry as she did her grocery shopping on Sunday. She thanked Sharon for the informative meeting and left. She would try chanting for Gaude's happiness. Maybe if he were a happy person, not the miserable, desperate smooth-talking con-man she had met up with, he would find honest work that used his skills of split-second timing, precision, and accurate aiming. For he did have skills. To pull off his stunt had taken *admirable* skill. He was adept enough not to do too much damage, yet caused enough injury to be rewarded by an insurance company. His aim and timing had been orchestrated so very accurately. She had to admit he was very good at what he did, even if it was a detestable, abominable criminal activity.

It certainly looked like he would get his reward. Hopeford seemed to want to pay him because it was cheaper than a lawsuit, going to court, spending days and weeks or months trying to prove a case that was not provable. They might have to spend a whole lot more money. Detective Miller said that the police operated by different rules than insurance companies.

As she drove to the market, Joy tried to clear her jostled brain. Once there she gazed at the marvelous display of colorful fruits and vegetables, trying to blot Gaude Velasquez out of her mind.

If only she could forget about him and go on with her life! Joy knew from past experience that chanting worked. It had helped her acquire her studio and her new truck.

She would chant as advised and hope for the best.

Chapter Nineteen

After going to the ATM on Old York after work, Joy stopped at the hardware store to get some gesso brushes. It was a bright, warm day after a deluge, and the sunlight was still lingering. While paying for her purchase, she saw the Eagle Rock newspaper, the *Boulevard Centennial* on the counter. She picked it up.

There was a photo of Todd's Drive-In on the cover. It had construction crews milling about and the windows were boarded up. Joy was oblivious to her surroundings, often living in her own "Art World," and hadn't noticed the drive-in being worked on. She usually brought her lunch with her and only went to Todd's, a couple blocks down the street, when she forgot, or didn't have time to make her lunch. Then she would order a bean burrito, a tostada, or a tuna sandwich on toasted rye bread with coleslaw "to go" and eat the meal in her studio.

Joy was shocked to see someone had taken "drive-in" literally.

"A fatal crash took place at Todd's, when a young college student lost control while making a left turn and drove into the drive-in, killing Mary

Posada and seriously injuring her son Wesley. Wesley was last reported at County USC Medical Center in critical condition with his father by his side.

"Police are still looking for witnesses that may have seen the accident, as it is unknown why the Acura lost control.

"The driver, the son of a local businessman, is known for being a world-class athlete and attending college. He was unable to tell the police what had happened."

Joy felt stunned. It occurred to her that the young college student might have met up with an accident stager, maybe even Velasquez himself. She remembered how hard it had been, during that first interview with Hopeford, to remember exactly what had happened. She would call Detective Miller at the Police Department tomorrow and suggest this scenario as a clue. If there was an "accident stager" involved, it would explain why the student lost control. Even if he were only tapped on his bumper, his lightweight Japanese car could have easily veered off its course and driven into the drive-in.

She felt horrified at reading about the fatality and the son's critical condition in the hospital. "That could have been me," Joy thought. She had sat down in the maroon vinyl booths at Todd's a couple of times and always near the window where she could keep an eye on her studio. Though it was a ways down the street, she could still see her place from the corner booth. Now she vowed never to sit in their booths ever again. She felt peculiar and haunted by this report. It turned her stomach. One life lost forever. One suffering person struggling to regain his life. It sounded like the college-student driver had regained all but his memory.

Joy had not lost control when she had met up with Velasquez. For one thing, she drove a heavy truck. So when he had smacked his vehicle against her, the truck hadn't veered off into the parked cars at the side of the road or gone up on the sidewalk and on into the buildings. She had remained steady at the wheel also. But thinking about it now in light of this report, she *could* have lost control. She *could* be in the intensive care unit of some hospital, fighting for her life.

Maybe chanting had protected her. Joy felt very lucky to have gotten away with so little injury.

The next morning she called Detective Miller.

Only the answering machine greeted her.

"Detective Miller, this is Joy Bravitsky. I don't know if this is relevant to the death at Todd's Drive-In, but maybe the driver met up with an accident stager. He lost control and can't remember what happened. There was a woman killed at the booth and her son is in critical condition. I just wonder if there is a clue here worth investigating. Feel free to call me about it. Thank you."

She would go over to Todd's and see if anyone could talk to her on the subject of this terrible accident. Her curiosity was pricked. If the driver had been an athlete, why would he lose control of his car? Athletes had to be extremely focused and aware of what they were doing. It just didn't seem like a chance occurrence.

Something happened that was wrong. Joy felt a peculiar uneasiness as if she knew there had been foul play. She needed to find out more to confirm her suspicions. *Was it just an accident?* Or had someone deliberately hit this college guy? Had someone tapped his bumper just enough to throw the car off into another angle, a change of direction that would lead the car to jump the curb and plow into Todd's place? It seemed very likely to her. Or maybe this was because she had met up with an accident stager herself? Maybe she generalized but still something seemed fishy. *Very fishy.* She couldn't shrug this off. It really bothered her, as if she were personally involved.

Another case of needing a witness. Maybe the police could locate one. She hadn't seen anything. Accidents were numerous on Old York. The street was dangerous. People drove way too fast, as if it were a freeway, when in fact it was a business street. The area was still run-down, still had a slight tinge of desperation. Artists had to survive in dangerous areas because they struggled financially. Downtown was worse. One of her friends had been seriously hit in her lightweight truck as she drove to get supplies. She had never fully recovered but had to rely on an electric scooter device to get around. Still, she came to openings at galleries, always with a smile on her face.

Another artist was attacked on the street in broad daylight by a man wielding a knife.

Joy had rejected the center of the city as a place to work as being too dangerous. Now she wondered if her little neighborhood was much safer.

In the morning she went down the street to talk to Russ, the owner of Todd's Drive-In.

"Good morning. I was wondering if I could talk to you about the accident that happened last month," she said to Russ, a robust and friendly man. Yet there was just a slight note of terror in his voice as he agreed. His anxious enthusiasm was tinged with nervousness. One of his customers had been killed.

She must have picked up an old paper. They had completed remodeling the restaurant during the month after the crash and it now looked very clean and modern. Instead of out-dated maroon vinyl booths with jagged holes fixed with scotch tape, there were light-gray tables and chairs, new and clean. White transparent shades covered the windows. The counters were now a clean grayish-white. Everything was light and airy.

"Yes, it took a month but we needed to remodel anyway," Russ smiled. "It looks much better now, don't you agree?"

"Oh yes, much nicer! But what exactly happened last month? What time of day did this crash happen?"

"It was about 4:20 in the afternoon. This young fellow lost consciousness or something and over-steered or lost control, crashing into the restaurant. No one seems to know exactly what happened. A woman sitting in the booth over there in the corner was killed. Her son is in the intensive care unit at USC. There were no witnesses. The driver wasn't hurt, at least he says he wasn't. That steel ATM stopped the car or it would have hit our order-taker, Lottie, who was standing right in back of it. Of course she jumped away and ran in the other direction, but who knows if she would have been fast enough? We replaced the ATM. Only three bolts held.

The fourth bolt came loose. The ATM saved the cooks also. We love that ATM!"

"Yes, I guess it's useful for more than generating cash!"

Russ laughed.

"You think it's possible that someone staged an accident, clipping the driver?"

"I guess anything is possible. The driver doesn't know what happened. He thought he lost consciousness, fell asleep or something. He had an injury from playing sports." Russ gestured with his broad hands. He was glad to tell his horrendous story. He needed to get it off his chest.

"Was he taking pain medication?"

"I don't think so. It's a mystery as to what exactly happened. No one knows since there weren't any witnesses. His father owns the auto-parts store up the street. The son was making a delivery. His car was totaled."

"My truck was hit down the street by an accident stager. I just wondered if someone clipped him, throwing the car off its course."

"I don't know. Maybe. I guess it's possible. No one knows and he can't remember. The police looked, but no witnesses were found. We saw it, of course! But too late to figure out exactly what happened prior to entering here. It's a mystery."

"Well, thank you for your information. Your restaurant looks so contemporary."

"Thanks. I thought they did a good job transforming it. The remodel was due anyway. We were stuck in the fifties!" Russ laughed nervously again. "The insurance paid for part of it. We paid for the rest."

"The vinyl booths were a bit of a throw-back," Joy observed. "This doesn't look like an old-fashioned diner anymore."

"Yes, we updated it. We thought of putting steel poles up outside to defend ourselves, but lightning doesn't strike twice in the same place." This statement was accompanied by a nervous gesture of wiping his hair back from his forehead.

"I guess poles on the sidewalk would help in some areas, but a car might hit in another part. They are quite inventive on Old York."

Russ laughed. "Well, I hope to see you here soon for lunch."

Joy went back down the street to her studio but felt dubious about the "facts" of this accident. For one thing, there *were* hardly any facts. What exactly *had* happened? No one seemed to know, only the results. They were readily apparent. A driver lost control, plowed into a restaurant, killed a lady and seriously injured her son. Russ had mentioned a couple of other minor injuries: the husband had a sprained ankle and a patron at the counter was blown out the door by the impact, injuring her wrist when she fell.

The father of the driver sold auto-parts up the street. The young son was making a delivery. He hadn't driven very far with his auto- parts delivery when he "lost control." It just didn't make any sense.

Joy scratched her head in disbelief. The story was honestly told. It just didn't reveal any picture of what had actually transpired. *Why had the young driver lost control?* Joy couldn't shake the feeling that something was very wrong. Maybe it was her sixth sense, but the sense of dread when she looked over at Todd's Drive-In was something she couldn't shake off. It was as if a skull-and-crossbones sign had been stuck on. She remembered, suddenly, that an artist had actually painted that sign on the plywood they had put up temporarily over the windows to cover the spider-web cracks of splintered glass. Yes, artists knew.

Joy had developed a sixth sense, a psychic awareness. Something *was* wrong.

She felt very sure of this, as if it were a fact.

Chapter Twenty

"We can go shopping for a wedding dress next week," Carey told Joy over the phone. Carey was excited and her voice trembled with anticipation. "Would that work for you?"

"How about Friday? I can take a day off just for you!"

"Thanks! That would be fine. I'll pick you up at the studio around ten in the morning."

"What an exciting time for you. I'm sure Stan will make you very happy."

"Oh, he's a wonderful man. He'll keep me laughing."

" I'll see you then." Joy smiled as she hung up the phone. It was great to have something to look forward to in life. She could shrug off the bleakness of accident stagers for a morning, shopping for Carey's wedding dress. They would find something wonderful!

Joy went back to her painting. She was tackling large canvases again. Large canvases were her favorite as she could really move in sweeping gestures. Painting for her was like modern dance, only she performed in the privacy of her studio. The canvas was evidence of her performance.

This canvas was six-feet by four-feet. Though the study had some vivid colors, intense yellow-orange and vivid magenta, there was a lavender-grayness that tamped down its tone. The mixed emotions Joy was feeling came through from beneath the layers of paint.

Many layers would be scumbled and glazed before she would be satisfied with the result. Many weeks, even months could pass until Joy got the results she was aiming at, however subconsciously. Since there was no map except for her study, the trial-and-error process, disquieting and uncertain, would have to be endured. Yet this was the thrill of painting—not being certain of the outcome. Chance, accident, luck, timing, energy, skill, all played their roles in every painting she executed. It was a contest, even a battle.

On Friday morning, promptly at ten o'clock, Carey arrived at the studio. "You've been busy!" she observed while looking around. "I already love the new one you've begun."

"It's a good start, anyway. We'll see how it goes. Anything can happen and usually does!"

"Listen, Stan and I want to buy a large painting when we get our new house. We don't want you to give it to us as a wedding present, we want to buy it."

"Oh, thank you! I can give you a smaller work as a present. You can pick it out."

"That would be very nice. But let's save that for another visit. We have a mission for today's schedule."

"Where are we going to start?"

"I thought downtown in the Garment District."

"Yes, that's where the Traffic Central Police Department is."

"Well, they have great clothes there too and at wholesale."

"We'll concentrate on your wedding wardrobe today. Forget the police!"

Joy offered to drive. Carey got in the truck, Joy jumped into the driver's seat, and they went around the block and headed for the freeway. As they drove down Old York, Joy pointed out the spot where Bravitski had been hit by Velasquez.

"How's that going?"

"He hasn't gotten any money yet. It's been almost four months. I just keep writing letters. The police report came and I sent that in. It says it's a "staged collision by sideswipe." I think the proof is there, except there were no witnesses."

"Hopeford should *not* pay him."

"I hope they don't. It will only encourage him to go out and stage another accident the next time he runs out of money. Maybe hit *me* again!"

"He wouldn't do that, would he?"

"I wouldn't put it past him."

"He endangered his own children. I don't like the sound of it."

"Yes, he seemed to be a cold, cruel person. I hope they pin it on him."

"What did the insurance detective say?"

"He agreed. 'Not a nice man,' was what he said."

"Just your luck to encounter him."

"I suppose there was a reason. There's a reason for everything. Perhaps he needed someone to expose him, someone who wouldn't be just an easy mark."

"You're tough. Probably he was surprised by your resistance."

"I guess I don't look tough. I've had to be as an artist fighting it out for my survival."

"You've survived!"

"Yes, that, for an artist, is a feat in itself!"

"You'll get back your success, I know it. The secret is being able to stick it out."

"Yes, I'm determined to get it back, all the success I had with beginner's luck. It's just a question of how to survive until I do. And actually I realized the other day at Disney, working with that attorney to acquire art for her office, that I like working with the collectors directly. When a gallery sells the art, the artist rarely meets the collector, let alone sees the environment where the work will reside."

"Yes, there are definite advantages to being your own dealer. The problem is finding your future collectors, I suppose."

"It does take time to socialize. But even Andy Warhol did that."

They arrived at the Garment District where colorful clothing hung outside the stores. "Let's ask where the bridal shops are," Carey said, as Joy found a place to park with a meter. They got out of the truck and Carey fished around for coins.

The two women entered the first shop they encountered. Rows of skirts and blouses, jeans and sweaters welcomed them. "Do you know where the bridal shops would be?" Carey asked.

"Just down the street there are several," a young, good-looking woman informed them. She was dressed in tights that stopped at her ankles, platform wedges, a short skirt of black leather, and a diagonal wrapped red silky top.

"Thanks," Joy said. They walked past more shops, T-shirts, bathrobes, brilliantly colored scarves, one could find any kind of apparel downtown. "I see the bridal shops," Joy said, pointing ahead. A mannequin modeling a white lace dress appeared in front of them.

"Do you think white is alright?" Carey asked.

"You've never been married. Of course it's perfectly fine."

"But I'm in my sixties."

"So what? You look forty."

"Thanks. Do you think lace is appropriate?"

"Yes, lace would be stunning."

"Even at the beach?"

"We'll find the perfect dress, I'm sure."

Joy and Carey went inside. Racks of beautiful white satin and lace creations lay before them. They were greeted by an older woman this time. She was very thin, almost brittle, and wore a black sheath with heels. "What kind of dress are you looking for?" she asked.

"I wear size nine or ten. I'm getting married on the beach, so something simple, not too long would be good."

"Let me show you what we have," the saleswoman commented, pulling out a breath-taking gossamer lace and satin creation. "This is mid-calf. You would wear white stockings. It would not drag on the sand."

"I love it!" Carey enthused. "Can I try it on?"

"Of course. The dressing room is over there."

Carey took the dress gingerly. It seemed like the perfect dress. It was the first one she saw. How could that be? Usually shopping took hours of trial and error. She was used to being frustrated on shopping trips. Could this be the one she would treasure?

"You've got a beautiful day for shopping," the saleswoman noted.

"Yes, it's great weather again, lots of sun."

The phone rang and the saleswoman clicked her heels as she went to answer it. Joy overheard that her name was Ellen as she talked to a potential customer.

Joy looked around as Ellen spoke on the phone. Would she herself ever get married? Somehow it didn't seem right for her. She had dedicated her life to her art just as a nun dedicates her life to God. Her art was the most important part of her life. A man might interfere. Joy mused about being single while looking at the tempting white gowns in the rack. They glowed with what seemed like an inner light.

Finally Carey came out. Joy sucked in her breath. Carey looked wonderful, every inch a bride. The dress eased gracefully over her torso, much of the bodice was lace, then tucked into a slim waist of satin. The skirt flowed in petal layers, a combination of satin and toile, past Carey's knees and about four inches beyond. The off-white, slightly ivory, was an iridescent mixture that enthralled Joy and seemed to light up Carey's face and blonde hair. Long sleeves flowed gracefully to the wrist, ending in a petal shape, echoing the layered skirt. It was lovely, beyond beautiful.

"I think it's just what we wanted to find," Joy enthused. "It looks terrific. It's stunning! Stan is going to be very pleased."

"Can you hold it for us?" Carey asked. "I think this is the one I want. But it's the first dress we found. We should look around some more, don't you think?"

Ellen laughed. "I'm sure you'll be back. This dress looks like it was made for you and your beach wedding."

Carey and Joy went to a few more shops, but found nothing to compete with the wonderful, gossamer creation they had found right off the bat.

"Let's find a place to eat lunch and then go back for the dress," Carey suggested.

Joy pointed to a taco place they had passed. "How about authentic Mexican food?"

"Yes, that sounds perfect."

Joy and Carey were able to sit outside under umbrellas. "Look, you can order fresh juices. How about the cucumber, lime and mint?"

"Wow, you really know Mexican."

"It's just that Highland Park is mostly Mexican. So I always say, 'Muchas Gracias.'"

Carey laughed. "And what else do you suggest?"

"Ribs with rice and beans is really good. And ask for corn tortillas, better than flour ones."

They ordered accordingly. As the two friends waited for their food, Carey suggested they find the bathroom. On their way to it, Joy blurted the newest worries out. "Carey, there was an accident near my studio. A young college-kid lost control of his car and drove into Todd's Drive-In. I have a hunch that this was a staged accident. The car killed a woman and seriously injured her son. I just have a weird feeling about it. Someone may have clipped him. The driver can't remember what happened."

"Did you call the police?"

"Yes, I phoned in my hunch to Detective Miller right away."

"What did she say?"

"She wasn't there. I left a message."

"Why do you think it was staged?"

"I don't know. It's just a weird feeling. The kid was a college athlete delivering an auto part for his dad down the street. I just think it's strange he should lose control. It was still broad daylight, around 4:20."

"Maybe you're right. Were there any witnesses?"

"No, that's just it. No one knows what happened."

"I wonder if there is a way to find out."

"Makes one want to carry a video camera around with them at all times!"

The two women returned to their seats. The waiter was just approaching carrying large platters of food. The tortillas were warm, wrapped in parchment. The beans swam in sauce. The ribs were boneless and tender enough to cut with a fork. The spicy food was cooled by the cucumber drink, which went down easily.

Soon they were quietly eating, enjoying their Mexican repast.

"No one might ever know. But I think your idea is quite plausible," Carey said as she cleaned the gravy with a tortilla, then stuck it in her mouth.

"I think you might be on to something."

Soon they were absorbed in eating their repast until their hunger was quenched. As Joy sipped the last of her juice she blurted, "Let's go back and get that beautiful dress! It's perfect on you. We wouldn't find anything more beautiful in Beverly Hills!"

"Yes, I love it!"

Carey laid her credit card on the table. "Give this to the waitress. I have to find the restroom. I'll be back shortly."

Joy watched as Carey left the table. At the next table an emotional conversation was going on. Joy couldn't help eavesdropping.

"I don't know, Mary. But something is drastically wrong. Shortie breaks down crying for no reason. In the middle of the night he wakes up screaming!"

"Rosie, that's terrible! What do you think happened? Can he talk about it?"

"He won't tell me anything. I ask him, 'whatever is wrong?' He just weeps!"

"Don't you have any suspicions? You must have some ideas?"

"It's that Gus Velasquez. Shortie lost his job as a mason. He said he was training with Gus, something about auto parts. Gus is, well I hate to say bad things about anyone, but…"

"Is that the guy who you believe stages accidents for the insurance money?"

"Yes, he's a creep and I think maybe a criminal. I suspect Shortie began something in cahoots with him."

"Is that how he makes his money now?"

"I don't know." Rosie began to cry. Big tears ran down her cheeks. She grabbed her napkin and began dabbing her face.

Joy glanced away, studying the menu. She had heard enough already. But Mary continued.

"You know people have been killed that way! Accident-staging is very dangerous. Do you suppose Shortie tried it?"

"That's what I am afraid of!" Rosie was still swiping at her face.

"Do you suppose he hurt someone?"

"I can't get him to say *anything*. How can I get him talking about it?"

"Fix an especially good meal. Get him comfortable. Then say, 'Is there something you should tell me?'"

Joy retrieved the credit card but in doing so she nervously swiped the guacamole dish with her elbow. It sailed across the table and landed on Rosie's dress.

"Oh, I'm so sorry!" Joy exclaimed. "Please let me pay the bill for dry cleaning. I'll give you my business card."

"Oh, it's really nothing. A little green spot."

"I insist. Please let me have your address and phone number."

"I'll write it on the napkin. I'll send you the cleaning bill. It's nice you are so generous and honest." She wrote her information on the napkin with a ball-point pen.

Carey returned. She took the credit card from Joy, who had been white-knuckling it, picked up the receipt and signed it. She hadn't noticed the tension in Joy's hand.

"Let's go back to that first shop!" Carey announced.

"I was hoping you would say that!" Joy laughed. She tucked the napkin with Rosie Garcia's address into her purse with a nervous gesture.

"I thought you would be back!" the shopkeeper Ellen enthused. "I already wrapped up the dress in layers of plastic and it's ready to go for you."

Carey took it and gave her credit card. "It's the right dress for a beach wedding. We're so grateful to have found it so quickly. And it fits perfectly."

"Yes, it was made for you in Heaven!"

Joy laughed. Carey *was* a heavenly friend. She had spent the day not just by herself for once. Though she liked to paint every day, friends were so valuable. She would skip a few days of painting to help her friends. They were one of the best things in life.

What a coincidence! Overhearing Rosie's conversation was certainly a lucky break. She would call Detective Miller the minute she returned to her studio.

This would be the best dry-cleaning bill she had ever paid.

Chapter Twenty-One

Once home, Joy printed up her caller I.D. She found upon perusing the print-out that "Picasso paintin" had called her! Although it was missing the "g", she had never been called by a painting before, and from a dead artist?

Stan always made her laugh. Maybe the painting was calling one of her canvases! What would a Picasso say to her paintings? "How do you do, you colorful thing, you. Let's hang together!" She laughed again. Just for the heck of it, she called the number. "The number you have reached is not in service," the taped voice said. "If you feel you have reached the wrong number, please consult the operator."

This didn't surprise Joy as the phone numbers he left rarely reached anyone. On a rare occasion that someone answered they would draw a blank!

In his secretive way, Stan was cheering her up again. Joy needed it. She imagined more dialogue between her canvas and the Picasso painting. "This isn't just a line. We could make beautiful art together!" This brought another smile to her weary work-worn face.

It was December, it had turned cool, and the rain had been heavy. The giant Chinese Elms outside her door were still dripping. The weather was overcast, and sudden thunder showers were predicted. Nevertheless, Joy planned a shopping trip for Christmas presents. She had made a few sales and had some money. Now she gathered up the mail from her box. There was a letter from Hopeford.

"Hmm," she murmured. It was exactly five months from the day that creep had hit her. She expected nothing but bad news from insurance companies. They had stopped helping her with various claims she had made. They used to be good but times had changed. Now they were only interested in profit. When she made a claim for a leak in her studio roof, they just sent out an "adjuster" who decided she hadn't maintained the roof correctly and denied her claim.

Hopeford's letter was just as bad or worse than what she imagined. It read:

You have been found liable for the accident you were involved in on July 13, 2010. We have paid the other party. For details call Agnes.

Joy's face turned red. How unfair! All she had managed to do with all her letter-writing and phone calls, even going to the trouble to get a police report, was postpone the inevitable for five months! The lawyer had scared them. Rather than investigate further, they preferred to hike up her insurance rate and put a black mark on her almost perfect driving- record. Joy was steamed!

Yet she knew it would happen this way. It was most predictable. Velasquez was an informed criminal. He knew what he was doing. He had it all down pat. Just hit her truck and collect the reward for his misdeed. It was all so easy.

At least this payment, however much it was, would get him off her trail. He could breathe easier. He got his money. He could buy his kids Christmas presents, *the kids he had intentionally injured.* "I bet they paid him for three kids," Joy muttered to herself, "when there were only two." She was aghast! She didn't get angry easily but now her anger knew no bounds. Joy wondered if he had beat up the missing child so he could take him or her to the doctor!

This last thought irritated her so much, she decided to call the Child Protection Agency the first thing in the morning and report Velasquez. She remembered that the police report had his address on it. She dug it out again from her files.

"Oh my God, he lives on the street just before Old York, one street North," she exclaimed to herself. "Oh, NO!" She would report him immediately. Fear took hold of her. Maybe he would try to hit her again when he ran out of money. She felt helpless against her own insurance company that refused to take her side even though she was their client. Unless she could produce a witness, Velasquez and his lawyer would win every time. He could just sideswipe her truck anytime he felt in need of cash. He could just claim he had the "right of way," and her insurance company would agree with him. Her truck would be his giant piggy bank! Although Detective Miller had assured her this would not be the case. She felt he wouldn't hit her again. Still Joy worried endlessly.

How could she protect herself against him? It just seemed completely wrong. She had a hard time sleeping that night, tossing and turning while thinking of this injustice. But finally she did fall into a troubled sleep.

The next morning Joy found the number for the Child Protection Services in the government section of the phone book. She dialed it immediately.

"I would like to report an accident stager. He steered his car into my truck with his kids in the back seat," she reported. "He had two kids in the car, though he claimed three—a toddler and a little girl around eight years old."

"Yes, we will take the report and follow up with an investigation next week. Do you know his name and address?"

"Yes. There was a police report. His name is Gaude Velasquez, and he lives on Medway Street just above Old York where my studio is located."

"Thank you for reporting this. Can we say your name?"

"Yes. I want him to know he can't get away with this. He probably thought I was the perfect victim, some stupid old broad who couldn't figure out his sleazy game."

"Yes, we will follow through next week to investigate. We will send someone from our staff out to his home."

"Can I follow the results?"

"No, we can't give out any information. But we will follow this up immediately."

"Thank you. I just think it's terrible that he can get away with this. My insurance company found me at fault because he has a lawyer and there were no witnesses I could find."

"Yes, they do that. Thank you for calling."

Joy hung up. Now Hopeford would put a black mark on her driving record and jack up her insurance rate. She might not be able to meet their demands for excess payments! Once again she would be victimized, this time by her own insurance company that had considered her a "superior driver" for almost all the twenty-seven years she had been with them. So much for "customer satisfaction"!

At least he should have given his kids some protection. What kind of father would intentionally injure his kids, even risking their lives? The little girl had not been belted in.

Joy's anger and indignation knew no bounds. She abhorred Gaude Velasquez, his risk-taking, his knowledge that he would win. He was a clever criminal that could have ended a few lives—hers for instance!

The victim role did not suit her. She shrugged as if to shake it off. But she had been forced into it. And now she was one. And there was no way out of it, just as if she had been straight-jacketed!

Gus's reward Joy learned, when she called Agnes the next morning, turned out to be the grand sum of eleven thousand dollars! He had been given two thousand for his "junk car," which he must have claimed as "totaled" (it had another dent besides the one further up and a broken tail-light was all). He claimed his personal injury at over five-thousand, while Joy had gone to one chiropractor visit for fifty dollars. He then got paid another four thousand for his "three" kids when there were only two in the car.

"We gave fourteen hundred to Juanita, twenty-five hundred to Jorge, and one-hundred for the baby," Agnes gushed. She sounded so sympathetic it made Joy nauseated.

"There were only two children in the car. I hope you realize your mistake."

"Oh, no mistake. We found you at fault."

"For what? Driving straight ahead?"

"You changed your story."

"I was in a state of shock. It took me almost a week to recall exactly what happened."

"It's too late. We go by your first report. We found you at fault. We never change our decision."

"You rewarded criminal activity. I hope you're satisfied. I'll send you the newspaper article the next time he hits and maybe kills someone."

"Well, I've got to go. Business, you know." Agnes hung up with her false cheerfulness.

Enraged, Joy just wanted to get rid of Hopeford. But would another insurance company be exactly the same? She distrusted all insurance companies now. What a racket!

Gaude knew what he was doing. Nothing had gone "wrong." But how about the accident at Todd's Drive-In? There was a death and another life hung in the balance. She was almost sure now that it was the work of Gaude's friend Shortie. Rosie, his wife, whom she had inadvertently met by spilling guacamole on her dress at the Mexican restaurant, had spilled the beans! She laughed at this unintentional pun. Then she called Detective Miller.

"It's hard to prove but thank you for the lead. The fact that Gaude Velasquez's name was mentioned as an 'accident stager' certainly is telling. But we can't pinpoint Shortie Garcia's strange behavior. It might be anything. He hasn't admitted to anything. However, we might send a detective out to question him using some other pretext."

"Yes, this should be checked out soon! They paid Velasquez and his three kids eleven thousand dollars!"

"I'm surprised. That much?"

"Yes, and he only had two kids in his car."

"People exaggerate."

Gaude seemed to have done this before. Joy had sensed experience, smelled it like Brandy had sniffed out the rats invading her kitchen. Yes, he had experience at accident-staging, she was sure. And since he was rewarded so generously, Velasquez probably would keep doing it. A lucrative, easy way to make thousands of dollars! Hardly any work at all! Would she be hit again? And if so, what would she, what *could* she do differently? There just didn't seem an answer. Joy had been driving as slowly and carefully as she had ever driven.

"What can I do to protect myself?" Joy asked Detective Miller. "Will he try to hit me again when he gets low on money?"

"I doubt it. You gave him a lot of trouble. How long has it been?"

"It took him five months."

"Well, I hope he has learned his lesson. We have his name and driver's license on file. We will watch his driving record carefully. If he is caught again, he will go to jail.

Accident-staging is a most dangerous crime. And we *will* send a detective out to interview his friend Shortie Garcia."

"But what can I do if there *is* a next time?"

"You should always carry a camera in your truck. Photograph everything, the damages, the license plate, the number of passengers."

"If I had photographs, it would prove that he is a liar."

"Yes, if he claimed three children when there were only two."

"What else should I do? What if he tries to hit me again?"

"I doubt he will do that. As I said, you proved to be a tough victim. These criminal types do not want any trouble. They do not want police reports, fights with insurance companies, reports to the DMV. They want to avoid the spotlight. They pick victims that they can easily extract money from. You turned out to be a fighter. He probably thought he would get his money in a week or two. It's to your credit that five months have elapsed."

"Well, thank you for all your help. I'll get a camera to carry around."

"Don't worry. Drive safely but don't get paranoid. If he selects another victim, we're on it! He probably had quite enough of you!

And we'll be watching Shortie too. You've done a good job. You didn't take it lying down."

Joy laughed. "Yes, I've been called a tough cookie. But I still lost the case."

"It seems like you lost. But you reported him. He may realize that he can't get away with this awful crime. Let us know if anything happens. We're here to help."

"Thanks. Bye."

Joy hung up. Her talk with Agnes at Hopeford had been revolting. But she really liked talking to Detective Miller. The Detective had taken time to explain the situation and seemed like a caring individual. She had gotten no concern or empathy from Agnes. Her supervisor, David Brenner, was the only person at Hopeford that had any brains. She would write another letter to Hopeford suggesting they give him a raise! Yet he had seemed powerless to change the absurd outcome. He had seemed to understand, yet there didn't seem to be a thing he could do to reverse their decision.

Joy would have to forget this horrible incident and go on with her life as an artist. There was plenty of good news in her life. Her niece Bridget would have her child in January, coming up very soon, as it was now the end of December. Her mother was doing well at age ninety. Her nephew Chris had found a girlfriend, Alice, a printmaker, whom he was dating. Carey, her friend, was getting married in the summer to Stan Moshan! Her Art was still selling, without an Art dealer despite an economic down turn.

Joy wouldn't let this incident pull her down. She might need another insurance company, though. Driving without insurance wasn't an option. The law was on their side. That case was closed. And it would be harder to find another company with this black mark on her record. Still, Joy counted her blessings. She still had her health and her beautiful little home. Joy would go to the studio the next day to continue painting.

Painting was her salvation in life.

Chapter Twenty-Two

Detective Marion Miller had worked her way up to Chief of Auto-Fraud. She was a meticulous investigator conversant with the law.

The Detective was a small brunette, lightweight, and she moved quickly about. Her brown eyes were intense, her chin pointed as if weighted with determination. Her nose was a bit large for her small face but it added to her look of authority. Her manner was brisk, but she was not a cold person. Despite her official title at the Police Department, people knew her as a warm, caring individual. However, she reserved little of that warmth for the criminals she encountered, often on a daily basis.

She had at first not returned Joy's call after the accident at Todd's Drive-In. Too far-fetched. Yes, it could have happened that the young athlete had been hit by an accident stager, bumped just enough to lose control of his lightweight Japanese car. But this scenario was a fictional construct unless there was definite proof. There had been no witnesses to help determine how or why the athlete had lost control of his vehicle and veered off onto the sidewalk and into the restaurant where the car proceeded to strike people. So Detective Miller had shrugged it off. Maybe Joy was psychic. Artists sometimes were. But at that moment, there was nothing concrete.

But now, by some lucky off-chance, Joy had overheard a conversation that led some credibility to this story. Tomas Garcia, nicknamed "Shortie," had a wife named Rosie Garcia who Joy Bravitsky had overheard talking in a restaurant, mentioning Gus Velasquez by name, referring to him as an "accident-stager." This clue was hard to ignore.

However, there wasn't enough proof to convict Velasquez or even interrogate him. There had been a slight accident that could have happened any which way. She had no proof Velasquez was somehow involved. However, she could fake it, questioning Shortie as if it were a fact.

This Shortie fellow needed to be questioned, first on some pretext, probably a standard canvas of the neighborhood looking for witnesses. She could send Donald Fraser out. He was good at digging out the truth. But thinking about Joy, whom she had come to think fondly of, she decided to do the job herself. She would call the Tomas and Rosie's home and set up an appointment. She checked the phone book and saw he was listed.

She picked up the phone immediately.

"Hello, is this Rosie Garcia? I'm Detective Marion Miller from the Los Angeles Police Department, Auto-Fraud Division."

"Yes. What is this about?" Rosie's voice was shaking.

"Nothing to worry about. We're just doing a routine neighborhood canvassing. Will you be home on Friday? We need your husband home also."

"What time?"

"We'd like to come in the morning. How about ten o'clock?"

"I'll tell Shortie. We'll be here." She hung up abruptly. Rosie's nervousness was hard to ignore.

Early Friday morning, Detective Marion Miller arose with a sense of determination and purpose that she had not felt as strongly for years. At ten o'clock, she would find out the truth about Shortie Garcia and maybe about Gaude Velasquez too, although she doubted that Shortie would turn out to be an informant. Usually friends were loyal and didn't reveal a thing. That was the tough part. She might get Shortie to break down but she still might not have evidence to arrest Velasquez. She sensed Gaude might be harder to pin down.

Velasquez hadn't killed anyone and the accident with Joy Bravitsky was still open to question and doubt. Nothing concrete had been proven. There was not a witness to confirm Joy's story, though Detective Miller believed it was true. Velasquez was smarter than Shortie, she guessed. He had done minimal damage and created soft-tissue injuries that made it all amorphous as to what exactly had happened. Successful accident-stagers were like Houdini; they performed a magic act of smoke and mirrors. The result was a fog-soup which defied explanations and facts. It was like pulling money out of the air. Insurance companies were in business to stay in business. They avoided expensive lawyers, lawsuits and court judgments. If there were no witnesses, accident stagers who worked with crooked lawyers and doctors and created minimal damage usually won. It was a rip-off of the public but there was not much she could do about it.

On the other hand, deaths were catastrophic; hard facts that brought accident-stagers out into the open where they were vulnerable. Deaths were an extremely serious crime that demanded intricate investigations. Collecting money illicitly by auto-fraud was one thing. Murder was altogether another. It put accident-staging into the high-crime arena.

Perhaps she could word it to throw Shortie off-balance. He would inadvertently give her the information she needed. How could she do this? The Detective could feel her brain revolving while reviewing what she knew and tried to find the right words to convict both of them. She was bringing Detective Fraser with her. He had experience extracting confessions. She would need his expertise.

At exactly ten o'clock, Detectives Miller and Fraser approached Shortie and Rosie's residence and knocked on their door. It was a small stucco home painted a faded pink with a few red roses on a struggling bush beside the steps. It looked like many of the other homes in the area, blending in. It did not look like the home of a criminal, but then what would a criminal's home look like? Detective Miller shook her head. No, criminals did not often display their activities but lived in a normal-looking environment. This home had low-wage earner written all over it. Her heart raced as she stepped back and waited, looking at the door; it's ugly, beige weathered wood that made her feel repulsed.

Rosie opened that door immediately as if she had been waiting nervously. She wore a plain, beige sheath cotton dress, as if wanting to blend into the wall behind her. Seated on the opposite wall in a recliner chair, Shortie appeared casually relaxed, not quite pulling off this attitude, Detective Miller noticed.

Despite the few signs of poverty, it was a homey-looking place. The detectives entered and found a large floral sofa to sit upon. The floor had a braided rug. A gray cat lay on a chair near a window where a shaft of sunlight made a triangle, so it could sun itself while napping. The furniture had many cushions thrown about making the house look cozy and comfortable. There was a large flat-screen TV dominating the living-room, the only modern-looking item in the house. Everything else looked dated and faded.

Detective Miller began by introducing herself and Donald Fraser. "We're here on a routine neighborhood check to find witnesses for the accident at Todd's Drive-In on November 12, 2010. As you probably know from the local paper, a young college student made a left-turn, lost control, and drove into Todd's killing Mary Posada and causing serious injury to her son Wesley who is still in a coma. As there were no witnesses found immediately, we are canvassing the neighborhood to find out if anyone saw it. The driver doesn't know what happened or why he lost control."

"We didn't see anything. You should try another house," Shortie replied, folding his arms defensively across his chest.

Rosie nodded her head in agreement but looked suspiciously at her husband who shrank back at her accusing glance. Detective Marion Miller observed this revealing sign.

"We think you know something because we found some evidence at the scene that may have connected you with the accident."

Detective Miller's white lie was aimed at gaining some ground, a toehold at the truth. She was stumbling in the dark, trying to catch hold of something tangible, she knew not what. To further the bluff, she took out a folder and "read" a clean sheet of blank paper, nodding authoritatively as she perused it.

"What did you find?" Rosie asked anxiously as she watched Detective Miller.

"We found a bit of metal that lay in the street, from a bumper. We checked it out and it matches the type of car you drive." She further consulted her "report." "A crush-factor is explored by accident reconstruction experts, as to damage to the bumper and the vehicle's body. These scientists can sometimes determine from the depth and angle of the dent exactly how an accident occurred."

She checked off some blank items on her white sheet of paper with her pencil, then stuck it in back of her ear, as if in readiness for her further report. "Can we please see your car?"

She was extemporaneously making this up. Her adrenaline made her heart beat even faster. Acting was a part of her profession; she had to believe she really *had* a report and act authoritatively. Detective Miller had to convince them that she already had enough evidence to convict him.

"O.K.," Shortie replied. He threw up his hands, then led them out to his car. The bumper was seriously damaged, although there was no metal actually missing. Her hunch had been correct enough. She breathed a silent sense of relief. Perhaps she had him!

Donald Fraser looked the bumper over. A sideswipe was very possible. "How did this happen?" he glowered at Shortie a bit menacingly.

"I hit a tree. I was drunk and lost control," Shortie lied.

"We think you staged an accident," Donald said, going for the juggler. "And Detective Miller has an official report she just referred to. You might as well tell us what happened. It's in your best interest to tell us the facts."

"I, I, I," Shortie could not get a coherent sentence out but seemed stuck on the first word.

"Where were you on November 12 at about 4:25 p.m.?" Detective Fraser continued the pressure.

"I was driving home, I..."

"Do you know Gaude Velasquez?" Marion Miller added accusingly.

"Yes, I," he still could not talk with any coherence. He began to blubber. "Gaude's a friend," he finally got out. "Just a friend!"

"We have evidence that Gaude Velasquez is an accident stager who makes his living hitting other drivers' vehicles in order to collect insurance money. Maybe he taught you?" Donald Fraser asked, playing with his badge as he spoke. The hard, shiny metal glittered throwing a glare of light on Shortie's face. It was a hunch he was playing. He didn't really have any proof, only gossip to go on. Nonetheless, he had to convince Shortie that he had a water-tight, leak-proof case against Velazquez. Had he succeeded? Had he hit the jackpot?

"Tell the truth," Rosie urged her husband who was now beginning to shake. "Tell the officers about your friendship with Gus."

"I" was all that Shortie could get out before he broke down into tears. He began to sob.

"Sit here and tell us everything," Detective Miller patted the flowered sofa with her warm hand.

"O.K." Shortie sat down. Tears were rolling down his cheeks and he gasped for breath. "I met Gus right after I lost my job— as a mason. Tomas was stuttering, something he never did. " I –I was a brick-layer and concrete laborer. I was an honest man doing hon-est labor with my hands. But after the job on the renovation of the tire store was completed, everyone was laid off. We did a great job making medical offices out of an old beat-up garage. It looks real nice now. Real nice." Shortie gasped for breath. He tried to calm himself down.

"I ran into Gus at the grocery store. He seemed like a very smart man. Maybe cold and conniving, but so smart! He suggested I learn his, well, his..."

"Go on," Detective Miller urged.

"He said that staging accidents was easy and lucrative." Shortie grasped his handkerchief and wiped his eyes. He took a deep breath.

"Gus said that after a couple or three times, I would have enough money to quit for a while. I only had to do a few hits a year. He said the insurance companies made it easy. I…" He broke down sobbing, grasping his handkerchief that was already soaked.

Donald Fraser took out handcuffs from the interior of his vest. "We have to take you into the Police Department now and book you for manslaughter in the death of Mary Posada. You may also be a suspect in the serious injury to her son Wesley. *You have the right to remain silent and to get an attorney.*" He placed the handcuffs on Shortie's wrist while Rosie looked on in horror.

"How could you? We weren't desperate! You could have found something honest to do. You have so many skills and talents! How could you ever imitate that crook Gus?"

Shortie gave her a pained look but said nothing as the two detectives led him away to the police car. Then Rosie began to sob. "How could you? How could you?" she wailed, watching her husband being conveyed into the back seat of the police car.

"Oh God, how could you?"

Chapter Twenty-Three

Gus Velasquez held tightly to the envelope from The Hopeford Insurance Company. It contained a check for eleven thousand dollars, the result of his original efforts plus five months of wrangling. He smugly thought about his prediction. Velasquez knew he would eventually win his case. Of course he would have to pay Mel Grant, his attorney, and Doctor Schuster, his crooked doctor. He called Dr. Schuster, Dr. Shyster, because for simple soft-tissue injuries he had given Gus a bill for five-thousand dollars to present to Hopeford. He would have to reimburse the good doctor half that amount. Still, after all his payola payments, Gaude would still have at least six thousand free and clear.

"I told Shortie I would win!" he mumbled to himself. He couldn't call Shortie with his victory story, however. No more meetings with him at the Brick Coffee-House.

He had read in the morning paper about Shortie's arrest for manslaughter. Gus shook his head. Shortie should have listened to him. All those lectures for nothing! Now Tomas was in jail and would probably be sentenced to major prison time, maybe Life. They probably wouldn't give him the death penalty. Juries were reluctant to kill criminals. The death penalty always was in question. Still, Shortie's life was now, in essence, ended.

Maria came into the dining room. She was dressed in his favorite gauzy flowered- print dress that clung to her curves and flowed with her movements. "Look at the generous check we received from Hopeford Insurance Company," Gus said, pulling the check out of envelope. He smiled at her admiringly.

"Wow! We'll have a great Christmas. We can shop at the mall this afternoon."

"You bet. I have to go to the bank now and do a few errands. Need anything?"

"We need another package of diapers for Juan."

"I'll stop at the drug store. I should be back in about an hour."

Gus left. He had managed to get the replacement Mercedes working tolerably. It still exuded a cloud of black smoke. The Air Quality Management Bureau might come down on him. However, it wasn't a crime, just negligence.

Gus wasn't gone very long when there was a knock on the door.

Maria answered it. A tall, red-haired lady with an identification badge on a gray, tailored suit stood before her. She looked official.

"Hello, I am Martha Taylor from the Child Protection Agency of Los Angeles. May I come in?" Her steely green eyes penetrated into Maria's brown ones.

"Yes, certainly." Maria immediately gave way. "My children are still sleeping. Why are you visiting? Did you want to see them?" Maria was appalled. She was a good mother, why should her parenting be open to question? What was a child-protection agent knocking on *her* door for?

"Yes, in due time. First, let me explain why I am here. Is your husband at home?"

"He went to the bank and is doing some errands. He'll be back in about an hour. What's this about?" She looked at Martha Taylor nervously. "Nothing has happened to my kids?" She began to feel extremely anxious, as if a blow to her head was about to fall.

"Yes, something *did* happen to them. They were in an auto accident."

"What? I know nothing about this! What accident? When?"

"On July 13, 2010, your husband's vehicle hit Joy Bravitski's truck. She has described it as a staged accident. There is a police report. Your husband was driving with two children in the back seat, a little girl and a toddler."

"He didn't say anything about this. Are you sure you have the right house?"

"Oh, yes. You didn't see injuries on the children?"

"Juanita was rubbing her arm a lot. And Juan cried in the bath-tub when Gus was bathing him. But now the kids are fine. I will go wake them up."

"Yes, let's talk to them."

Maria ran into the bedroom. "Jorge, Juanita, time to get up. It's almost ten o'clock." She went over and scooped up the toddler Juan. The child rubbed his eyes with his little fist. Juanita jumped up and grabbed a jumper out of the closet. Jorge rolled out of the bed, pushing a book he had been reading with a flashlight aside. He grabbed his jeans and began pulling them on.

Soon the two older children were seated at the table and Juan in his high-chair. Maria poured orange juice in short, wide glasses. "You can see they are all fine, hungry and ready for their breakfast. I allow them to sleep in on Saturday. On weekdays they get up at six. They need the extra rest on weekends."

"Yes, I see that you take good care of them. But your husband is careless."

"I can't believe he would not tell me about an accident! Was it his fault?"

"It was reported as a staged accident."

"What exactly is that, may I ask?"

"A staged accident is a phony accident planned to create a sit-uation where an insurance company will dole out money to the perpetrator."

"You mean a *deliberate* crash?"

"Yes, exactly. Someone hits another car with his vehicle to make it look like an accident so he can collect insurance funds from the other driver's insurance company."

"You can't be serious! Purposely hit someone? My husband would *never* do such a thing!"

"We think he did. And the police have him under suspicion. They are watching him for future collisions. We fear his children are in grave danger. Accident-staging is a precarious business, indeed. People, including children, have been killed."

"Mama, can we play outside today?" Juanita asked. She didn't want to talk about her daddy's accident, though she knew what the lady was referring to.

"Yeah, I want to go out," Jorge added.

"You need to have eggs and toast first," Maria insisted. "I will fix them for you in a minute."

"Yes, I will let you continue your morning, Martha told her. It looks like you take good care of your children. I'll return next week to question your husband. Here is my card. If you have any questions, please don't hesitate to call. If your husband is indeed an accident stager, we will need to remove the children from your home and put them into foster care. If your children are endangered, they cannot stay with their parents. I see no bruises on your children now but the accident happened five months ago. We are just worried that this scenario might happen again with tragic consequences."

"I'll talk to Gus. He is a good husband and father. I don't believe he hit anyone deliberately. He would never do such a thing! He does make money from insurance companies but told me he worked for them as a consultant. I believe him. But I'll try to find out if this awful thing you describe is true. I don't believe Gus would deliberately endanger the kids. He takes very good care of them. He cooks dinner, bathes them, drives them around..." Maria began to look anguished as she said this. Tears started to swell in her eyes. She shook her head as if to throw them off.

"No! I just don't believe he could possibly do that abhorrent thing. No! It's not possible! And I certainly wouldn't want you to take our kids away! I love our kids very much. Please go!" Maria face had taken on a tortured look as she tried to deal with her emotions. Yet the full truth about her husband had not taken root. She pushed the idea that Gus would hurt her kids out of her thoughts. She believed that her husband was a good man. Didn't he love his kids? She had never doubted his caring for them.

"Well, I'll be back next week. How about next Saturday at this time?"

"I'll make sure Gus is here." Maria tried valiantly to recover herself. She was outraged and had begun to shake. What was going on here? What would happen to her family? She gained a fragile composure, turning to speak more calmly to Martha Taylor.

"Thank you for coming out. I don't believe the children are in any danger whatsoever. But I'll try to find out."

Investigator Taylor nodded, walked back out the door, got into her silver car, and pulled away. Maria watched her in fascinated horror. She tried to think but her jumbled fears and incoherent feelings prevented anything logical. Gus! Could Gus be a criminal? No! Her mind refused to accept this. No one could be a better father! He spent an inordinate amount of time with them. She didn't know any other father who took so much time with his kids.

She tried to think back to last July. Yes, there *had* been something wrong with both Juanita's arm and Juan's body. Both children had slight bruises. Why hadn't she asked more questions? Gus was so very good at glossing things over. He had written it off as playground injuries. She had accepted this explanation. And then he had taken all three kids to the doctor. Why had he taken Jorge? Nothing was wrong with Jorge, was there? She couldn't remember any injury or soreness even. Once in a while he did beat Jorge. He resented Jorge's habit of reading so much for some reason. Envy? Gus hadn't been able to finish his law education because of her pregnancy.

And how about Gus's car? He had that old white Mercedes. He had said he was trading it in. Was there a crash? He hadn't mentioned anything. He brought home a light green one that spewed smoke. The white one had a dent and a broken tail-light. She hadn't asked any questions. Why had she kept silent? Why had he traded in his car? He hadn't gotten a better one. This car was worse!

And what exactly did he consult with insurance companies about? Maria wondered why she hadn't ever gotten him to talk about his job. And what if he was an accident stager as Martha Taylor had accused him? What could she do? *She would not be able to trust him with the children ever again.* She would have to move out and take her kids with her. A foster home would not be right! No, she would never let it happen! Her kids had a father. Her kids had a mother. They had a home, a normal life like any other normal kids. Why would Martha Taylor want to disrupt this life? She felt a vacuous emptiness, like a hole in her heart. Her mind raced furiously, trying to readjust to this abhorrent new reality.

Was Gus honest? He was a rapid smooth-talker. She had admired this trait in the past. He could win any argument. He always knew better. He was always "right." She accepted his explanations and perhaps his obfuscations. *Was he a criminal?* She just couldn't accept it. No!

Just as she had this thought, Gus pulled his Benz into the driveway. Although only a half-hour had passed since Martha Taylor had left, Maria's view of Gus's personality had undergone a major downward shift. Now she felt suspicious of his activities, whereas before she had always trusted him. She watched anxiously as he took out the bag with the diapers and strode with his long legs toward the door.

"Ready to go shopping at the mall?" His smile drooped as he looked at Maria's horrified expression. "What happened to you?" he asked, astonished. "You look like you saw a vampire!" He let out a high-pitched laugh, trying to joke her into a better mood.

"A Martha Taylor was here from the Child Protection Agency. She said some pretty awful things. I don't know what to believe, Gus. She wants you here on Saturday to question you."

"What awful things? I can't believe this! What right does she have to come here with accusations?"

"She said you are under suspicion of being an accident stager by the Los Angeles Police Department. You were reported by someone you hit, Joy Bravitsky. Why didn't you tell me about this accident. *Was* it an accident?"

"Oh, you mean last July. No, I didn't hit her on purpose. What are you saying? She came out of the post-office without looking and we had a fender-bender. No big deal. I didn't even think it was worth mentioning to you. Not wanting you to worry. It was nothing."

"What do you mean, nothing? You had an accident and didn't even tell me? The kids were in the back seat, injured, and you wanted me not to worry?"

"I told you it was nothing. If the kids had been seriously injured, I would have certainly told you! What do you think I am?"

"I don't know what you are, Gus! I thought I knew you. I thought you cared about your kids." She began to sob. All the tension and misery she had felt for the last hour suddenly broke loose.

Hearing their mother's grief, Juanita and Juan began to cry. They had been in the kitchen grabbing a snack. They ran into the living-room where they saw a heated verbal exchange between their parents. Confused and frightened, Jorge ran to his room.

Gus grabbed Juan and put his arm around Juanita before they too could flee. "I certainly do love my kids. Can't you see? What are you accusing me of?"

"Oh Gus, I'm so confused. I don't know what to think. I don't know anything about you."

"We've been married ten years. You should know me by now."

"I *thought* I did," Maria attempted to control herself. She stifled her sobs. "I certainly thought I did. I thought you were honest."

"Look, I can explain everything. Let's drop the subject for now. We can talk about it later. Let's take the kids to the mall now.

We can enjoy the afternoon, the holiday spirit, see the decorations, go shopping, have lunch in the food court. Maybe we can even see a matinee movie. There is a huge, decorated Christmas tree at the Americana Mall that everyone is raving about."

"I don't know, Gus. I don't think I'm up to it. I've got to think."

"Well, I'll take them then."

"No! I can't trust you with them."

"What do you mean? I'll be careful. They'll be fine. I'm going now. Come on Jorge, quick. We're going to the mall." He turned toward the children's room, and commanded Jorge to come out. Jorge slowly appeared from the bedroom looking extremely pale. Gus took Juanita by the arm while carrying Juan, urgently motioning to Jorge to follow, and raced out the door.

Maria sat down hard on the chair. She would have to think about what to do next. Leave Gus? I just don't know what to do, she thought. I just don't know...

She sat in a stupor for some time. She stared at the grandfather clock and stupidly watched the hands go around. They seemed to be pulling her with them farther into a void, a black hole where nothing made sense.

It was unbelievable! Gus lied to her about the accident? Or he just didn't tell her? Wasn't that the same as a lie? Was it on purpose or a fender-bender?

The fact that he didn't tell her was suspicious. If it had been a real accident, wouldn't he have said something? And what exactly was that large check from Hopeford for? Was it a claim for injuries? Gus just told her it was nothing. *Nothing would not have gotten eleven thousand dollars!* Insurance companies were not so generous. No! Something was drastically wrong.

She must leave Gus and take the children. Shouldn't she do that? Her mind raced to try to figure out her options. The children must never go to foster homes. No! Never!

She didn't endanger her children. Martha Taylor, if she gave Maria a choice, would allow her to take the children and leave Gus, wouldn't she? She began to sob again at the thought of leaving Gus and disrupting the family.

But what if Gus were innocent? What if it *was* just a fender-bender? What if this Joy Bravitsky lady had come out of the post-office without looking? Was there any proof of accident-staging? She stopped crying. She had to get a hold of herself. One last sob and she began to dab her face with a handkerchief.

The house was quiet. Without the kids or Gus's non-stop banter, the house became a tomb. As she sat looking without seeing the grandfather clock, the silence bore down on her like a mallet hitting her head. Without her family, Maria realized, she had nothing. There would be nothing. She would feel nothing. She would be nothing! Whatever could she do?

She badly needed to talk to someone. Who could she call? She needed to get someone else's opinion. Her frantic thoughts churned in her feverish mind. Suddenly she remembered Rosie Garcia, Shortie's wife. She didn't know Rosie very well but had talked to her briefly a few times. They both had kids and Shortie worked with Gus. Surely, Rosie would know more; maybe she could tell her the truth about Gus? Maybe she could shed some insight into this baffling situation.

With the thought of calling Rosie in mind, Maria poked through Gus's desk, finding his old, black phone directory. She quickly found Shortie's home number. She picked up the phone and punched in the numbers.

Rosie looked at the ringing phone wondering who it could be. She didn't feel like talking to anyone but answered after two rings. "Hello. What do you want?"

Maria was struck by Rosie's defensive manner. But she went ahead bravely. "This is Maria Velasquez, Gus's wife. I don't know if you remember me. I…"

"You have a lot of nerve calling me up! You and your sleazy husband are responsible for this mess! My husband's terrible situation is all your fault! Go to Hell!" And Rosie slammed the phone down.

Maria was taken aback. Her hand shook as she replaced the receiver. What had happened to Shortie? Maria hadn't time to read the morning paper between her family and her job. Was there something in it? Whatever had happened to Shortie? Gus hadn't mentioned anything. She feverishly began to hunt for the newspaper but Gus must have taken it or thrown it into the trash barrel outside.

Maria sat back down stunned. If she knew what happened to Shortie, maybe it would shed some light on her problem and whatever happened with her husband. Another fifteen minutes passed in desolate silence. She couldn't bear it. Her heart was heavy with a sorrow too encompassing to withstand. This situation had to be cleared up immediately. *She had to know the truth, however painful it was.* Finally, Maria, at wits'-end, tried Rosie again.

"Hello."

"Listen, I don't know what happened." Maria was talking fast, spitting out her words. "Gus didn't tell me anything. I'm innocent. Don't blame me! I'm just a mother of three kids. I have a job working for Senator Black. Gus told me he was an insurance consultant. Please, please don't hang up on me! Tell me what happened." Maria had spoken so rapidly, she now gasped for breath.

"Shortie is in jail! And Gus is responsible! He taught him accident- staging!"

"No! I thought they sold auto parts."

"Ha! That's a good one. No, they drove into other people's cars to collect insurance money."

"I can't believe it. No, it can't be!"

"Well, it is. Shortie hit a college kid making a left turn. The kid drove into Todd's Drive-In killing a woman at the corner booth and putting her son in a coma!"

"No, No, No!" Maria started to sob. She clutched the phone as if it were a life-preserver. "I'm so sorry. Oh God, I'm so, so sorry!"

"Well, it's too late now to be sorry. *Shortie will probably spend the rest of his life in prison.* If he had never met Gus Velasquez, my husband would be here with me now, and the woman and her son would have walked out of the restaurant and continued their lives."

"Oh, God!"

"Don't you monitor your husband? *Don't you even know what he does?*"

"Gus told me he was an insurance consultant and worked with Shortie selling auto- parts. I never doubted him."

"He's a criminal! Your husband is a God-damned criminal!"

"No!" Maria sobbed. "No! Gus? A criminal?"

"Yes, and he took Shortie in for the ride."

"I'm so sorry. I do apologize. I did nothing. I knew nothing."

"Well, wake up and smell the coffee. I'm through with both of you!"

And with that she hung up, leaving Maria tightly clutching a dead phone.

Chapter Twenty-Four

"This is extraordinary! The Getty Museum, no less! You've just got to put this in your calendar." Joy was bubbling over as she talked to Carey over the phone.

"You're being honored at the Getty? Oh, how fabulous! What's the occasion?"

"Remember, I told you that Lyn Kienholz was asking for slides of paintings I did in the seventies?"

"Vaguely, yes."

"Well her new book is finally out after four years of effort. And the Getty helped with the funding."

"Have you seen it?"

"No. Sample copies will be at the party. It's an encyclopedia-like book with five-hundred artists. Probably the photos are post-age-stamp size."

"So when is the celebration?"

"It's on Thursday at seven. Can you come with me?"

"Are you kidding? I wouldn't miss it for the world! The Getty. You and the Getty Museum!"

"It should be great! They are serving food, so you don't have to worry about dinner. The Getty has gourmet fare."

"Can't wait. By the way, I am almost finished with the screen-play, *Mixed Messages*, so we can have a double celebration. Stan says some producers are interested!"

"Oh, that's fabulous! Tell me everything on Thursday. I want to know all the details."

"See you then. I'll drive. Pick you up at the studio. How about six o'clock?"

"Perfect."

After her telephone break, Joy went back to her crayon draw-ing. The drawings were evolving, becoming more complex. This one had two light blues and two whites—turquoise contrasted with sky blue, and iridescent white contrasted with chalk white. There was also a little chrome green, a grayed olive color. As she layered the crayon, gesturing to Bach's *Brandenburg Concerto,* Joy thought about this new move in her long-faded career. Would the book make any difference? Would it help pull her career up from the abyss it had fallen into? Or would her struggle remain the same? Months upon months of not knowing where her next sale would be coming from, with no show in sight? Joy wondered about the hard life she had chosen.

Hopeford had doubled her insurance bill, just as she had pre-dicted. She had paid it twice but knew she would have to find another company. It was just impossible to pay three-thousand dollars a year for car insurance! She had been calling around and going on the Internet but as yet had not found a company that would insure her truck for a reasonable amount of money. They all told her she had just had an "at fault" accident. Joy had tried to explain the situation but they told her it was on her record. This made her angry; the unfairness of this judgment-call against her.

Jose's tow-truck was once again started up. Joy heard the roar-ing engine and cringed. Walking over to her gate, she could see there was no one in the idling truck. That jerk was probably at the corner market already, getting a beer.

Her aggravation increased. Why didn't this dude start his truck when he was ready to take off? He still ran his truck "warming it up" for half an hour, as if he had parked it in Iceland, even after she had complained for almost a year. *She began to cough* as the fumes poured into her studio. If she yelled at him, it would only increase his obstinacy. Meanwhile, the dirty exhaust spewed into her studio and onto her canvases. She tried so hard to keep her studio clean, sweeping and mopping it every week or two. She was so sick of this fight that she could never win. It reminded her of her battle with Hopeford. Would Thursday ever come? Her problems would dissolve at least for one evening.

But Thursday did come around. Promptly at six, Carey drove her blue Chysler up to the studio door. Joy had gone home to feed Brandy and changed into her new favorite color, chartreuse. A yellow-green jean jacket covered a light-olive silk tank-top. Silk shorts made of collaged men's silk ties by Sue Wong and dark green tights completed the outfit. Sue Wong was a designer who borrowed from artists's paintings. In return, she had welcomed artists into her design studio to select from her sample racks. Joy still had clothes she had selected at discount years ago. These clothes never went out of style and were always creative and comfortable to wear.

"So what's happening with your screenplay?" Joy asked Carey as the city, with its flash of lights, moved past her. The night was clear and the black sky was diamond- studded with stars and an airplane blinking light sparks.

"Stan says there's a good chance a producer will option it. He's got a lot of friends in the industry. He loves the screenplay and would like to star in it."

"He's a terrific actor. He's hilarious!"

"Yes, I think he'd be perfect. I'm so excited!"

Joy and Carey arrived at the Getty's driveway and were told to drive all the way up the hill instead of parking at the bottom lot and taking the tram. A long line of cars preceding them winded around. "I've never driven this far up. Is there another parking lot at the top?" asked Carey.

"I haven't a clue," Joy responded. "This is a first for me too. I usually take the tram."

Five minutes later, Richard Meier's sleek modernist white buildings loomed ahead. These massive structures were enhanced by Robert Irwin's maze of gardens to the west side.

"We can go to the gardens later. See them in the moonlight!" Joy exclaimed. She was ecstatic. The Getty never failed to transform her mood. She couldn't help smiling.

They found the higher parking structure. "I didn't even know this lot existed," Carey said. "We must be going to a very special event."

"I don't know. We'll see when we take a look at the book." Joy was apprehensive. She hadn't gotten a proof sheet or any e-mail preview of what her work would look like in the volume. It could be awful, for all she knew. She cringed.

L. A. Rising! Carey laughed. "Stan calls it Joy Bravitsky Rising, he's so sure it will help your career."

They entered the pavilion. So many of her friends had made the book! Yes, her friends, her contemporaries, she suddenly realized were "has-beens" or "would-have-beens" just like she was! All of us waiting for our "second-coming!" she mused. We who have become dinosaurs, waiting for our "comeback," whenever that might be, if ever.

Joy began to talk with her old friend Craig. He had put her in a show in the nineties he called "Color Consciousness." Later that year he had been in a museum group show. She had been proud of him and attended the reception. They were pals, artists on the rise. There had been a flow, a movement for both their work. Now where was the activity? She hadn't seen a show of Craig's in years. And there was her old friend Don from Art school. He was a terrific painter, spending as much as a year on one work. Don also made paint, grinding his own pigments, and she had benefited from his expertise and used his products. Now where was he? She hadn't seen any of his new work in years.

"Hello Don, isn't this great? I'm so glad to see you here!"

"You too! Congratulations. Let's have lunch next week and catch up. I'm listed in the phone directory. Please call."

"Oh, I'd love it! I'll definitely look you up. I was just wondering about you."

There were five or six sample copies of the new book on the circular counter some distance away. She wanted badly to look but at the same time the anxiety she felt kept her talking to her old friends. Carey took the initiative.

"Let's go see!" She pulled reluctant Joy by the arm.

It was excruciating to Joy to have to look at her own work. Her critical sense was fine-tuned. Nothing she did ever looked "good enough" to her. And here it was exposed to public view, for the whole world to see.

"Oh, look how lavish it is!" Carey exclaimed turning the pages. Joy, afraid to look, finally glanced at some of the illustrations. "Oh!" was all she could utter.

"The Getty put hundreds of thousands of dollars into this book," Guy observed. He was looking at another copy next to their's. He was an excellent sculptor who had found a way to keep his career going. It *was* possible.

"Wow! I wondered if it would be an encyclopedia with postage-sized reproductions. But look at this! There is a whole page for every artist with two giant reproductions of the work and two critical essays."

There was a reproduction of a *Black Forest* painting, one of the series Joy had done for her German grandparents who had died of starvation and disease in the German Concentration Camp, Bergen-Belson. Also reproduced was *Blue Branches (for Van Gogh)* that had been in her first show in New York City at David Fine Gallery. It had sold to a woman who was to become a museum director, when she brought her mother into the gallery to acquire it.

The reproductions couldn't have been more elegant. The glossy photos showed the paintings to the greatest advantage possible. The two critical reviews were positive and one was poetic.

"I'm thrilled!" Joy exclaimed. Her relief was overwhelming. There was one copy for the artists to sign their page. Joy waited until it was her turn. She and Carey found her page and with a flourish, Joy put her signature on it. This was a proud moment in her life. The reproductions she had so worried about were absolutely beautiful. Stunning!

The release of her anxiety made Joy hungry. The disaster she had feared was averted. She couldn't have been prouder. "Let's get something to eat." There was finger-food spread out buffet-style: small boiled potatoes with colorful toppings and smoked salmon on pita bread with dill. Carey and Joy picked up napkins, then filled them with delicious tidbits. They were soon engrossed in eating their fill.

"Life should always be like this. Why are there so many unsolvable problems and frustrations?"

"A kite flies higher against the wind," Carey pointed out. "You did very well. I believe you will get some calls and maybe some sales from this. Who knows what this type of exposure will lead to?"

"I hope you're right. I need all the help I can get."

After eating they walked in the gardens. The maze Robert Irwin had designed for the Getty was filled with flowers and trees, ferns and vines, a riot of growth disciplined to fit the circle. In the center was an Indian tee-pee-like structure of steel poles adorned with climbing plants and flowers. The moon illuminated their iridescent shimmer. Joy felt as if she had flown temporarily to heaven. Gazing at the moon, she realized that her problems were miniscule. She was doing what she loved and now was getting some real recognition for it. All the struggle, rejections, poverty, frustrations and disappointments had suddenly vanished, as if a magic wand had transformed her life into a garden.

"Carey, life is good! I admit that without the struggle, my life would be vapid."

"Yes, we always think that maybe if we win the lottery, we'd be really happy to sit around doing nothing. But it doesn't work that way."

"The Buddhists state that happiness comes from overcoming obstacles," Joy noted.

"I think they're right. Creating something from nothing is my favorite activity. I would be terminally bored without my creative life. Nothing else gives me as much satisfaction. Except being with Stan, of course."

"Yes, Stan. The wedding will be spectacular."

"We'll pick out that painting soon. You're a star!"

"Maybe not a star, but perhaps I have risen out of the mud a little tonight!"

Carey laughed. The two friends joined arms and headed back to the parking lot. It had been a full, lovely evening.

"Oh, if life was always like this," Joy sighed.

Chapter Twenty-Five

Martha Taylor knocked on the door of Gus and Maria's home precisely at ten o'clock as she had promised. She had also called to confirm her visit.

Gus himself answered her knock. "Come right in!" he cheerfully greeted her.

Maria, sitting on the sofa, was dressed in a somber brown suit. Her face had a grim, determined expression. The children had been bathed and wore clean clothes. Juanita sat at attention, the full skirt of her pink dress spread carefully out around her. Jorge had on clean jeans and a T-shirt that said, "I'm a cat-person" with a drawing of Garfinkle below the lettering.

Juan had on an Osh-Kosh bib-jumper in blue sear-sucker, and he had a red lollipop in his hand, still wrapped in cellophane that he beat on his high-chair. He had a grim expression, as if he knew what was going on.

"Mr. Velasquez, after a week of investigation, we have determined that you are endangering your children. We cannot leave them in your possession. I talked to Maria over the telephone this week. She has agreed to take the children back to Mexico to live with the children's grandparents. We would like you to sign some papers I have here." She withdrew a fat folder from her briefcase and a pen from her purse.

"What do you mean? I don't understand." Gus looked stricken. He turned a pale whitish-green.

"The police report has determined that you stage accidents. Not only do you endanger yourself and other drivers, you take your children with you and injure them."

"Yes, there was an accident. But it wasn't intentional, no siree!"

"There's evidence to prove the contrary, I'm afraid. We can't have you endangering your children again."

"But this is false! Utterly false! I've had a few accidents, yes. But they were just happenstance, not on purpose! Everyone has their share of accidents. Tell me anyone who has a perfect driving record."

"We don't need a perfect record. But you have been found to *intentionally* cause accidents to collect insurance money. Fraud has been shown. We can't have you driving around with your children in the back seat, crashing into unsuspecting drivers so you can talk your way into collecting injury and damage awards. You use your children, your car, and yourself to cause suffering and injury to yourself and others. The State of California now demands the children be taken away from you to a safe place."

"We're leaving you, Gus." Maria said simply. "We cannot stay with you. I'm sorry." Her face was stiff with determination.

"No! I will not let you go!" Gus turned on his heel and dashed over to Maria and the children. "I cannot let you leave! You and the kids are my life, my love, my reason for existing!"

"Then why don't you care about their safety?" Maria demanded, glancing at her children who headed for the bedroom as quickly as they could.

"I care! I really care! This is wrong!" He turned with a red-faced, angry look to Martha Taylor.

The Inspector became frightened. She tried to keep her cool and addressed Gus in a professional tone. "I'm sorry. But this was the decision. I will go now. I'll check periodically. Maria has given me the address in Mexico. I will follow this case up." She turned quickly towards the door.

Suddenly Gus exploded. He ran to the door and blocked Martha's path. His face was brutally vivid with anguish. He caught her tightly by the wrist before she could make her hasty retreat. She felt a sharp pain as he gripped her arm like a vice gripping an iron rod.

"You can't do this to me! I won't allow you to take my kids away from me. And my wife too! Who do you think you are, coming to my home and disrupting my family!?"

Martha Taylor managed to press the button on her cell phone with her other hand. She had pulled the phone out, just in case. The red button automatically rang up the police. From her past experience she knew that doing her job had its dangerous moments. Crucial to continuing her life without injuries was having on hand a way to notify law enforcement when a tight situation arose. Although she felt in danger, Martha would talk calmly and professionally to Gaude Velasquez whose red, angry countenance faced her now with a most threatening expression.

"Mr. Velasquez, I am a professional merely doing my job. There may be a probation period you can work toward. If you stay calm, we will walk you through the various options you may have. Right now, the decision has been made. But it may be temporary. You have to demonstrate your ability to be a father who does not harm his children or others, whether they be in your home, your car, or on the street."

Gus's face remained red. He did not loosen the vice-grip on her arm.

"I can't let you take my kids away from me. I can't let you convince my wife that I'm an unfit father and allow her to go back to Mexico with them. Don't you see? Can't you see how very much I love and care about my family?" He gripped Martha's arm even harder.

Martha winced. She was beginning to feel hot, shooting pains racing up her arm.

"Please unhand me, Mr. Velasquez. You are only making this harder on yourself. I didn't make the final decision. I only make a recommendation. A committee met last week and made the final judgment. Your behavior in attacking me will only work against you. If you will, please let go!"

"No! I will do no such thing. You're the person who is ruining my life! The committee, whoever they are, only took your recommendation. They are following your orders."

Martha Taylor tried to remain calm until the police could arrive. She must talk softly but firmly to him. Her wrist ached and she could feel a bruise beginning to well up.

"Please let go. You are only hurting yourself. This situation may be temporary. Your behavior will be taken into consideration."

"No! You cannot do this to me. You cannot take my family away from me!"

Suddenly the door pushed open behind Martha Taylor. Three armed policeman shoved their way in, pointing their guns ahead of them. Immediately, Martha was pushed out to the safety of the front yard, as Gaude, in a state of alarm, let go of her. She grabbed her wrist in pain and looked through the open door at the proceedings. Gaude had grabbed one of the policeman's arms and was wrestling with his gun.

Maria raced toward the bedroom while screaming, "Gaude, don't resist! Give yourself up! Don't fight with the police!"

"I'm not afraid of anybody!" Gaude yelled while frantically attempting to wrest the gun away from the officer. He managed to get the policeman's arm down when suddenly the gun fired hitting Gaude's foot.

"Oh, Oh!" Gus plunked down on the floor hard in a sitting position, grabbing his foot with both hands. The blood began oozing from beneath his sock. He grabbed his shoe and, after loosing the ties, removed it and threw the shoe across the room.

One of the other police officers took out his handcuffs, and walking behind Gaude, he grabbed his arms, pulled them back, and clicked the cuffs onto Gus's wrists with a forceful motion. The three officers then worked as a team to pull their suspect up and carry him, hopping on one foot, to the police car. He was howling in pain and anguish. On her cell-phone, Martha Taylor called an ambulance.

Officer Julio Gonzalez put his gun back into his holster. He would talk to Maria while the other officers stayed in the police car watching over Gaude until the ambulance arrived. He thanked Martha Taylor for her quick work. Then he turned to Maria.

"Mrs. Velasquez, we're so sorry for this injury. He will be taken to County USC Hospital and put in the jail ward. He'll probably need surgery to remove the bullet. If he hadn't resisted our arrest, he wouldn't have gotten shot. I'm really sorry it came to this."

Maria was sobbing. She couldn't say anything.

"He'll be alright. This is just a wound. The other officers have put a tourniquet on his foot to stanch the blood. He'll be fine. The surgeon will remove the bullet. It will take your husband a few weeks to recover his strength."

Maria tried again to speak. But no words came out.

The siren of the ambulance wailed in the background.

"You saw we had no choice. The gun went off because your husband would not submit. He refused to cooperate. He wrestled with my arm. It went off accidentally."

Maria looked at the officer, wiping her eyes. "I told Gaude to submit. I screamed at him. He is so obstinate. But I don't believe he deserved to be shot!"

"I'm really sorry. Accidents do happen when there is resistance. We really try to be sure the process of arresting someone doesn't result in harm."

"Please, let me be. Please go away."

"We'll go as soon as the ambulance arrives. We anticipate it at any minute."

He looked out the door. The wail of the ambulance came closer, then died down, as the red paramedic truck parked in front of the house. Red lights blinked their shadow on the wall of the living room. Gaude, crying out in pain, was lifted from the police car with the aid of all three officers and put on a stretcher. The head paramedic nodded and the police withdrew, still watching. Gaude's stretcher was carried to the ambulance and shoved in. Quickly the rear doors were locked; the driver went to his door, opened it and jumped in. It was all fast, smooth, efficient effort.

The wail of the siren blasted out, the ambulance took off, erasing the blinking red light from the walls, leaving them forlornly blank.

Maria watched the proceedings with feelings of anguish and sadness, beyond what she had ever experienced. She felt Gaude's pain but at the same time hated him with a vengeance. She had been duped, all these years, thinking she married an honest man who loved his kids. She felt tricked, victimized, taken advantage of. Her trust in him had been betrayed. Maria felt rage whenever she thought of him. Her life had been destroyed.

"Thank you, Ma'am, I'll be leaving the premises now," the policeman said tipping his hat, interrupting her reverie. He had come back into the house after the paramedics left, though he did not know what to say to Gaude's poor wife. It was best just to leave, he figured. He quickly stepped outside, closing the door behind him with a soft click.

Maria sat stunned for a few minutes. Then she remembered her children who had hidden in the bedroom, scared to come out. She went to the room and found them huddled together, Juanita and Jorge hugging baby Juan. They were frightened to death of the commotion, the gunshots, their father's screams of pain.

"It's over," Maria said. "It's going to be fine. We're going to move to Mexico. We'll start packing tomorrow. For now, let's go for a walk. How about some treats from the bakery?" She gathered up her children, put on sweaters and made sure they had shoes, and soon they were walking out the door together holding hands.

A chill, sunny December day greeted them. Though the tumult of the morning refused to leave their minds, life must go on.

It was time for them to begin a new life, a life in a different country without their father.

Chapter Twenty-Six

Disappointedly, no results were conjured up instantly for Joy's work and her career from the new book. The phone remained silent.

"It's going to take a while," Carey consoled her. "You'll see things pick up when the book gets into circulation. Also, you can use the book *now* to create some movement."

"Yes, you're right. I have to do it myself. Milton Berle said, 'If opportunity doesn't knock, build a door.'"

Carey laughed. "Others will do it for you soon. But, for now, it's your job."

"So how's the screenplay?"

"It's definitely been optioned. Stan is in talks for the leading man. We're trying to tempt Meryl Streep to play the leading woman."

"She's fantastic! I hope you get her. I think she'd make a great pairing with Stan."

"Yes, they both have a comedic streak to draw upon."

"It's a comedy?"

"Oh definitely. A romantic comedy."

"I can't wait to see it. Can I read your screenplay?"

"Do you want to? Of course!"

"I'd like to write for the movies. I wrote for the school news-paper in college and got a job from that at the local newspaper. I wrote an Art column."

"You could probably write a movie. You can do anything!"

"Well, not anything. I can't figure out how to get the phone ringing again."

"Be patient! The book just came out. It will take time. But it will help you a lot! Your work looked great, very photogenic!"

"Your word in God's ear!"

"We'll get together soon. Got to get back to work."

"Take care."

Joy hung up. She took a walk to the local market for the morn-ing newspaper.

One headline fixated her:

ALLEGED ACCIDENT-STAGER SHOT IN THE FOOT BY POLICE- OFFICER AFTER RESISTING ARREST FOR INJURING CHILD-PROTECTION AGENT.

Gaude Velasquez, 42, of Highland Park, was arrested yesterday when he resisted and fought with Officer Julio Gonzalez after injuring child-protection agent Martha Taylor. Ms. Taylor suffered a bruised wrist when Velasquez grabbed and held her. In the ensuing shuffle between Gonzalez and Velasquez, the officer's gun went off, hitting Velasquez in the foot.

Velasquez is suspected of belonging to a ring of accident stagers that includes Tomas (Shortie) Garcia, 40, who was recently arrested as a sus-pect in the left-turn accident where a college athlete lost control of his car and drove into Todd's Drive-In. The car struck Mary Posada, killing her, and also hit her son Wesley, putting him into a coma.

Both men are being held for questioning. Garcia is already at the downtown Men's Correctional Institution. Velasquez will be brought to this institution after foot-surgery at County USC Hospital. Tomas Garcia will be brought to trial for the charge of Involuntary Manslaughter. Detective Marion Miller explained that accident-staging is an extremely dangerous crime. She would like to warn the public to keep a camera in the car at all times.

Joy had suspected the truth, yet had questioned it as just instinct. Now she felt astonishment at her guesswork being so close to the facts. So it was a cohort that had caused the accident at Todd's hamburger joint. Was Gaude an instructor, teaching this Garcia fellow how to strike others for profit? The whole idea made her feel nauseated. Gaude was in the hospital with an injured foot. "I guess his karma caught up with him," Joy mused. He wouldn't be able to stalk her, at least for a while, and the silent phone calls had stopped. The news should have made Joy feel better, but she only felt repulsed and sickened. Accident- staging was a desperate, horrendous crime. And how about the children? Joy was still in a state of shock that he had taken his children with him. He didn't deserve to have children!

After a while of this brooding, Joy took out a new canvas she had stretched. A glue sizing would be applied as the next step. She had made the glue the night before at home, soaking the crystals. In the morning she heated the jar in a double-boiler until the swollen crystals dissolved, stirring with a chopstick. She then took the jar to the studio for her morning's work. Now she scrubbed the glue into the canvas weave with a stiff scrub-brush. It was better to throw herself into her work than think about Gaude Velasquez.

This was work Joy usually allocated to an assistant. But Val was not around. He had contracted Cancer and had taken leave from the full-time job he had found. He had offered to return to work for her a few hours a day. "Just concentrate on getting well," she told him. "Rest, exercise, and carrot juice will help you. You can do it!" She did not want him straining himself in any way. Assistant work was not hard, just time-consuming. Still, Val needed to rest and preserve his energy for getting well.

Throwing herself into the menial labor, she even found enjoy-ment. If she concentrated on this busy-work, her problems dis-solved, at least for a while. There was nothing like working to distract herself from issues she would like to put off thinking about. Worrying about the economy and lack of sales would not help matters. Joy was doing her best. She determined to focus on the task at hand.

She finished scrubbing in the glue and while letting it dry, began the study for the canvas. She had already cut the paper to match the proportion of the canvas. She decided on black-and-white for this painting. Layering only black-and-white produced a dramatic canvas. Rubbing the black crayon created ominous shadows. It would suit her mood.

Taking out a thick, greasy black crayon, she forcefully glided an arc vertically down the stark, white page. This was followed by another arc opposite it, curved toward it, with a thin, black crayon. She swiped across both arcs with a soft paper towel in sweeping motions, blurring the lines. She then reached for the iridescent white oil crayon. This she wielded tightly, cutting horizontally across both arcs, with a sweeping motion. She cleaned off the black oil wax that had stuck to the white crayon, picked up from the cross-hatched line, with a paper towel. Taking her palette knife, she scraped across the white, revealing some of the black. All this was done on the floor, the paper lying on a Masonite board.

Enough of a start had been made. Now she put the sheet up against the wall on another Masonite board. She then attacked it with her black and white crayons, her absorbent paper towels, her palette knife, and even her fingernails. Soon she was engrossed in violent stabbing, dotting, rubbing, slashing-weaving the wavering lines into a watery whole. She was a dancer, a fencer, a toreador. All her anger, her joy, her love exploded onto the page. After half-an-hour of this cathartic expulsion of her feelings and energy, she felt exhausted. Her sky-light shot beams of natural light onto the crayon, making it sing. Close-up, the texture of the crayon caught the light, giving it an iridescent glow.

Joy sat back to look at the whole work. The drawing needed some pencil lines, some more chalk white crayon, and a few more iridescent white areas. The iridescent white came off as a pearl white, a contrast to the chalk white. She proceeded to attack the paper again with the crayons, pencil and rag. Gestures were made with her whole body, not just her wrist. Again and again she attacked the paper. Her hands now held four thick crayons. As quickly as she could, she grabbed the different whites, the mars black, the ivory black and slashed lines and areas. Her energy shot out in a frenzy of movement and gesture. Non-stop for two more hours, she slashed, scraped, wiped and smeared the crayons onto the paper. The glorious whole began to coalesce. Parts were coming together, weaving a bit of poetry and inspiration into a drawing.

At lunch time, Joy put the crayons down and went over to the stretched and now sized canvas. Testing it with a finger, she found it was dry. After lunch she could put the first of the many coats of Gesso, sanding in between layers.

She thought she might try Don before lunch. She dialed operator assistance and wrote his number down. His answering machine picked up.

"Hi, Don. This is Joy Bravitsky. It was lovely seeing you at the Getty after all these years! Your paintings looked tremendous in the book. I would love to have lunch with you. Please call soon." She left her phone number. Joy felt a little disappointment that he had not answered. Leaving messages wasn't her favorite option. So often people didn't call back. It would have been nice to have a lunch with Don on her calendar.

She took out her sack lunch, bottled water, and a book and prepared to take her break. The phone rang, cutting welcomingly through the silence. It was Don!

"When would you like to come over? There's a Chinese restaurant near here in Culver City. It's healthy, interesting food. Do you like Chinese?"

"One of my favorites! Yes! How do I get to your studio?"

"Take La Cienega south to Washington Boulevard. Turn right. I'm before Culver. He gave her the street address on Washington.

"Got it. How about Wednesday?"

"Sounds good. See you Wednesday at twelve?"

"I'll be there. I can't wait to see your studio!" It was only Monday, the start of the week. But at least she would have a mid-week break from her work, something exciting to look forward to.

Joy was enthused. She felt comfortable with Don, an old friend all the way back from Art school. It wasn't exactly like a date. Was it? She hadn't been on a date in years.

She called Carey. "Guess what. I almost have a date!"

"What do you mean, almost? Is it a date or what?"

"It's a lunch with a man, an old friend. Remember Don at the Getty? He's such a wonderful painter."

"I do. That large hulk of a man. He resembled a big bear."

Joy laughed. "Yes, he looks like a dock-laborer. But he's as fine a painter as you could ever want to see."

"How long has it been since you had a date?"

"I can't even remember! It's been so long. Anyway, this is just a lunch with an old friend."

"When are you going?"

"This Wednesday."

"Well, let me know how it goes. By the way, I read an article in the news this morning that they caught two accident stagers."

"Yes, they shot one in the foot! It's the guy that hit me with his kids in the back seat. I guess his karma is catching up with him."

"He deserved it. He'll recover but I hope he learned his lesson! Did you ever find a new insurance company?"

"Not yet. I'm still researching on the Internet."

"You're a good driver. You deserve to be treated well. I thought the way Hopeford treated you was disgusting. After twenty-seven years of superior driving, they acted like you were a fraud, accusing you of changing your story, and telling you it was your fault!"

"I hope they read the article. Come to think of it, I'll make a copy and send it to David Brenner. He was the only one who believed me."

"Yes, do that! You got the last laugh."

"I'd laugh, yes, but it's just *not* funny. Killing and injuring people is not a joke. I still get a stitch of pain once in a while in my right knee when I climb the stairs. Just a reminder what a detestable criminal he is!"

"Well, it's over. You can relax. Got to go! Stan is taking me to lunch at Milton's."

"Have a good lunch. And say 'Hi' to Stan for me."

"Will do. Have fun with Don."

Joy hung up. For years she hadn't thought twice about men. She had concentrated on her Art. But it was nice now to have a lunch to look forward to. She felt her life was swerving to the right track again.

Back to as normal as an artist's life could get.

Chapter Twenty-Seven

D on's studio, when she found the parking lot at the back and walked into the space, was cavernous, light-filled, and crowded with gigantic stretched canvases. The paintings, two in progress, were multi-layered, out-of-phase, vividly colored shapes that jostled and melded into each other. The eye roved in multi-directions, caught in a tangle of color in motion.

The studio was lit by large, clerestory windows and three large skylights that let the natural light waft in and settle softly on the canvases, illuminating them. The whole studio seemed to glow with color and light.

Don walked toward Joy extending his hand. "Glad you found my studio. Welcome!"

"This is awesome! Are these commissioned works?"

"Yes, two of the twelve-foot canvases are for Pepsico in Upstate New York. The others I am doing for myself. Pepsico pays very well."

"I know. They bought an oil on paper from me years ago and asked if the price was 'all I wanted.'"

Don laughed. "I'm using cell-vinyl colors. I make the paint myself," he gestured to machinery in the back. "I also sell the colors I grind by hand, as you know."

"Yes, your paint is excellent. I now use oils, though. I like Old Holland tubes but they're so expensive."

"Pigments went up in price this year. Paint in the Art store is outrageously priced. That's one reason I decided, years ago, to learn how to make it myself. That's when I bought the equipment you see, grinders and mixers." He pointed to a mass of greasy black machinery in the back.

"So do you have any shows coming up?"

"I do. Not in L. A., however. I'm having a mid-career retrospective in Miami at the Contemporary Art Institute next year. I do want to include new work, though many collectors have already been notified and generously agreed to lend paintings."

"Will it travel here?"

"We don't know yet. San Francisco has expressed some interest in it. I did have a gallery there. I showed at the *SFMOMA Artist's Gallery.*"

"Yes, I showed there too. Until they kicked out all their non-Bay Area Artists."

"The new Director's policy. I did quite well there with Sally and Marian."

"So did I. Definitely, I miss the enthusiasm for my work in San Francisco. I just got a call from an appraiser asking for the value of the *Black Forest* series paintings one of my collectors owns. She bought it from *SFMOMA.*"

"Like the one in the new book?"

"Exactly."

"Those are stunning paintings. You came off very well. Better than most."

"So did you. Your paintings are extraordinary, just great!"

"Thank you. But how about if I clean up and we go to lunch?"

"That would be perfect. I'm starving."

Joy was soon driving Don in her truck to the Chinese restaurant. Don said his car was too cluttered.

"Low mileage," Don muttered.

"Oh no, I bought it new."

"You must be doing alright."

"Yes, I was before the economy tanked and galleries dropped me, I dropped them, or they went out of business." They were passing a row of non-descript shops. "Do I keep going straight?" Joy asked.

"Yes. Go through that light and then make a left." Don pointed ahead.

"The gallery-artist relationship is tough. I was with *SFMOMA* for thirty years." Joy noted.

"Same here," Don agreed.

"Galleries move, go in a 'different direction,' show dead artists or what they term 'secondary market.' Joy winced as she spoke the word "dead."

"I agree with all of the above. It's all happened to me." Don nodded in agreement.

"I got the Pepsico commission through an artist friend who got it from an Art Consultant!" Don gestured with his large hands.

"You have to get sales any way you can!" Joy enthused.

"Do you have any shows coming up?" Don inquired.

"Right now, only a bird-sanctuary auction I painted a screech-owl for." Joy admitted shrugging her shoulders.

Don laughed, a loud booming sound. "I'd like to see it."

"The owl is bluish-purple with large eyes, the pupils rimmed in yellow-orange. I worked from a photograph in a bird book. The owl is startled by the photographer. It raises its wing to defend itself and looks startled, almost cross-eyed."

"That's hilarious!"

"The auction is the day after my birthday in May. You're invited."

"Are you working on any abstract canvases?" Don asked.

"Yes. I'm using black and white. I've done a study for a five-foot canvas. I use paint-stick, oil crayon, pencil and oil paint."

"Easier to sell smaller sizes."

"Certainly. My gestural approach is best on very large canvases but I've learned to work smaller. Last year I sold several that size."

"There's the Chinese place," Don pointed to an airy looking place with large glass windows and lots of potted plants.

Joy found a parking spot in back of the restaurant. Don got out and opened the driver's side door for her. Inside the eatery, orange and red lanterns hung from the ceiling in a festive atmosphere. They were shown to a table by a Chinese man holding a stack of dark-red menus.

"What's good here?" Joy asked when they were seated.

"I like the stir-fried spinach with ginger and garlic. They also have a good lemon-chicken. Also the tofu with asparagus and bitter melon is very delicious with brown rice. And the special today, I noticed when we walked in, is cod stir-fried with green and red peppers and onions."

"Maybe I'll have the special. Sounds good."

"I'm going to have the lemon-chicken. I've been hungering for it all morning."

"That sounds delicious too."

"Would you like to share a pot of green-tea?"

"Definitely."

The Chinese man reappeared and they ordered. "I guess he is the hostess and the waitress both."

"He's also the cook."

Joy laughed gaily. She was having a good time, she had to admit. She had been awed by Don's huge studio. Now she was laughing and enjoying herself. Don wasn't handsome or dressed impressively. She noticed, however, that he was wearing some new jeans that were still stiff and clean. No paint spatters whatsoever. She wondered if he had bought them for her visit.

The food came, steaming hot and fresh. They ate eagerly and in silence. Joy felt comfortable with Don. He was a terrific painter who had found a way to continue, even though there was an economic recession and paintings, especially abstraction, seemed to have gone out of style.

"I'm glad you're able to find places to show so you can continue painting," Joy finally observed after clearing half of her plate, washing the food down with the green tea.

"It isn't easy. Who knew Art would be at the mercy of fashion?"

"But it always has been. Remember Rembrandt? He went bankrupt when jewel-tone colors became the rage. And Van Gogh shocked people with his bold, vivid colors. He died considering himself a failure."

"Yes, you're right. What I'm doing isn't 'in', but fortunately some people still love abstraction."

"It would be easy to give up. But I'm too much of a coward to shoot myself in the head like Van Gogh, or even to cut my ear off!"

Don laughed. "So what else is new in your life?"

"I fought with my insurance company for five months. A man named Velasquez hit my truck to collect insurance. He claimed he had the 'right-of-way' when he deliberately side-swiped me. The shocking thing is that he had his two kids in the back seat. The sleaze-bag even claimed he had three!"

"He has an artist's name! So did he win?"

"Yes, to the tune of eleven-thousand dollars. Claiming his two kids, a toddler and a little girl helped him get more money. He even claimed a third child that wasn't in the car at all! I guess he had him in the trunk!"

Don laughed but then his face turned angry.

"What a creep! Insurance companies are milquetoasts. They just want to make money! He had a lawyer, I suppose."

"That's how he won."

"No witnesses?"

"There was one but I didn't stop to talk to him. Velasquez did, however."

"Next time you'll know better. Were you hurt?"

"My knee got wacked sideways. It's not a big deal. I sometimes still feel a twinge when I walk up stairs. I have twenty-five steps up the hill to my house."

"Glad you weren't hurt worse. He'll receive his just punishment from the Universe. All you have to do is avoid him."

"Yes. I just got the news that the police shot him in the foot!"

"That's justice! When someone goes out with the intention of harming others for selfish gain, he shoots himself in the foot. Only, in this case, a police gun did it for him!"

"Yes, that's so true!" Joy laughed.

"Shooting yourself in the proverbial foot, or actual foot, is one thing. But to take children along! That's abhorrent!"

"I reported him to the Child Protection Agency. A woman came out to take his kids away. He fought with her and the police came out. That's when a gun went off by accident, hitting him in his foot. I read about it in the paper."

"So that's his karma."

"Yes, it's cause and effect. The Buddhists believe it always comes back to you, positive or negative causes that you make."

"So is he in jail?"

"Yes. He's under arrest though he's probably in the hospital. I guess he will be there for a while. Then he goes to prison. Not too long, however. He only hurt her wrist when he grabbed it too hard. And they haven't proven he's an Accident-Stager."

"Just watch out when you drive. People are desperate. The unemployment rate is sky- high. Be extra careful."

"I'm trying. I've become a paranoid driver."

"So what else?"

"My mom turned ninety! We celebrated in Reno. I drove up with my nephew, Chris."

"My mother is ninety also. She has a boyfriend who drives her around."

"Oh, that's terrific! Is she healthy?"

"Yes, thank God."

"How about yours?"

"She's doing fine. Mother wins at bridge that she plays three times a week. She also walks around the park near our home." Joy smiled in relief. Her mother was an important part of her life.

"She sounds strong."

"I think she's the strongest woman I've ever known!"

"How about sales. Any luck?"

"Yes, I sold an oil on paper to an attorney at Disney!"

"Your work is excellent. You need to keep plugging."

"Yes, perhaps the book will help."

The all-in-one waiter, host, and cook came with the bill. Don picked it up. "It's on me."

"Thanks for lunch. It's great to see your studio and the new work!"

As they left the restaurant, Don put his arm across Joy's back. He opened the truck door for her after she electronically unlocked it with a click. Joy felt serene and loved. She hadn't had a gentleman in her life for years. This was wonderful! She felt so comfortable with him. Joy would definitely see him again if he wanted.

She drove Don back to his studio. "Do you want to come in for tea?" he asked.

"I've got to get back to my painting. But I'd love to come back to see the commission before you ship it to New York."

"That will be at least another month."

"Perhaps we could get together before that. How about a visit to my studio?"

"I'll have to see. I want to finish the commission. How about if I call you?"

"That will be fine. Good-Luck with it."

"Thanks! It should work without a hitch."

Joy watched Don walk back to his studio. She was proud of him. He had found a way to continue painting, even in the void created by the economy and fashion. Yes, it was possible! He inspired her to throw herself back into her work. There was hope, after all.

And it was nice to have a date after years of being alone.

Chapter Twenty-Eight

"So, how did it go?' Carey asked over the phone. She was still seated at her computer writing the last scene of her screenplay. Her little home offered a view of apricot and peach trees through the side window. A cup of tea was perched on a saucer to her right.

"Don's a great guy! And he's working on big commissions—twelve foot paintings for Pepsico. He also has a mid-career retrospective coming up in Miami." Joy was still at her studio, though the light was fading. It was Thursday, the day after her lunch with Don. She had waited as long as she possibly could to tell Carey all the details.

"Wow! Guess it's possible even at your stage of career."

"I don't think I'll be stuck forever. I never have been before. There was always a show somewhere."

"Probably the economy doesn't help. And painting has been 'dead' for years."

"Yes, graffiti is 'in'. Conceptual art is big. Cartoon art in painting is what they are showing. Take off your clothes. Party as Art. Anything goes!"

"Photography also is very 'in.' Easy to understand."

"If you do serious work and stick with the evolution of your work, bucking trends, you just have to wait it out."

"Some curator will catch up with you."

"That's the only road. It's a long, long, lonely one, however."

"I don't think the galleries understand what you're doing. Galleries now want a certain 'look'. Anything outside of that draws a blank for them."

"It wasn't that way when I started back in the seventies. Galleries looked for good artists, good work, not trends."

"Well, it's their loss. Are you going to see Don again?"

"I invited him to my studio. He's really busy with all his commissions and the retrospective right now."

"So when is he coming over?"

"I don't know."

"Well, I have great news! Our movie, *Mixed Messages,* is going into production!"

"Oh, that's terrific!"

"Stan is so excited. He's playing the lead!"

"He'll be great! You said you would let me read the screenplay?"

"I'll bring it over to your studio next week. Stan wants to pick out a painting for our new home, wherever that will be."

"Wonderful! What day would be good?"

"Probably Thursday. I have to confer with Stan."

"Thursday would be fine. I have new paintings to show you."

"I'll call you tomorrow."

"Thanks."

Joy went back to working on her drawing. It was almost finished and would make a good study for the canvas she was preparing. She would start the coats of gesso, sanding in between each layer until a smooth marble-like surface was achieved.

Joy still felt like an outsider. The art world had managed to push her out; now they seemed to be on the fence about her. But pushing further "in" seemed almost impossible. No one seemed to understand her new work. Aside from the bird auction, there was no show planned. She had gone to several galleries in search of a show, but no one seemed to care. One after another, they had rejected her work. It shouldn't feel personal. It was, after all, the painting they were rejecting, not her. But it *did* feel very personal. Joy supposed if she hadn't had what a friend called "her run of success," she would not feel the difference so brutally. But the stark contrast between trying to keep up with the demand of galleries and collectors and having no demand whatsoever was steeply stark. It was like trying to run up a steep hill with roller skates on. She was always going to the galleries with hope, optimism, and a friendly smile, and one-by-one they implied she was just another hanger-on, desperate for a show, with work they would reject.

The book should have made a difference. One collector had asked her to autograph her page. But she didn't buy any more work. A gallery, however, did ask her to submit work for their computer files for "projects." That was a step forward. The gallery was spacious and well-located. It was a gallery she had hung around for a couple of years, bringing in actual work and going to openings, trying to get her foot in the door. The Gallery Director, however, told her his schedule was full for the next two years.

One of his artists had even recommended her. Still the Director hadn't budged. He told the artist, "I have no plans for her."

But the book *had* accomplished something. She had gotten her work into his computer, if not his gallery. She would just have to be patient. *She was tired of being patient.* But there seemed to be no alternative. This was the most interest she had been able to conjure up.

The phone rang as she was brushing the first coat of gesso on her new canvas.

"Joy, it's Gary."

"Hi, Gary. What's new?"

"Mother fell and couldn't get back up. Ellie, the nurse she walks around the park with, took her to St. Theresa's Hospital.

She had a CAT-scan. They found nothing wrong and her vital signs were good. They gave her a walker."

"She needed one. She's been complaining her legs and feet are swollen."

"She retains water."

" No, that's not the problem. I believe she has Gout. Remember her ankles were always swollen?"

"Well, the walker will help. She can get around again without falling."

"Was she hurt in the fall?"

"Just a bump on her head."

"I'll call her."

How could she go on without her mother? Amy was the only person who knew her completely, who never wavered in her faith about Joy's eventual success. Amy was her best friend, her confidante. The long letter that was written to her each week confirmed Joy's devotion. In return she received the news each week from Amy: her bridge success (she almost always won), her friends, the family update. Her struggle would be void without Amy's support and love.

"Hello. Amy? How are you?"

"I don't feel well. This is the end. I'm too shaky and weak. I'm too weak to go on."

"You were fine only a few months ago. You must stop taking the diuretics that doctor put you on."

"But my legs are so swollen! I can't even walk. It's useless!'

"Mother, you have Gout. Cherry juice will help you more than any pill."

"Gary wants me to go to assisted living."

"That would probably be best. Remember how you always wanted to go to Classical Residence? You said when Dad's life ended, you would move where your friend Wilma went. She loved it there!"

"I don't want to move. All my clothes and furniture are here. And that place is so expensive!"

"This is probably what you need now. Perhaps when you get your strength back, you can move back home."

"I guess you're right. I just don't feel good. I can't even walk. There's no hope. I've lived too long."

"Mother, we need you!" Joy choked back a sob. She would save her tears for later, after hanging up.

"It's too late. Bye."

Joy started to cry but caught herself and dialed Gary's number instead.

"Hi bro. Mom's not well. She thinks this is the end!"

"I've made arrangements for her to go to Astrid House. It's a new assisted living home in the mountains. It's quite beautiful and well-managed. I've already checked it out. I'm on this. She needs twenty-four- hour care right now. She can't walk by herself. Living alone is just not possible for her right at the moment."

"Oh, she'll love it! She'll fit right in. She's very social and will make new friends. Glad you're right on this."

Joy paused, then urgently added, "We need to get her off diuretics. It's weakened her. Can't the doctor see that it's not the right medication?"

"We'll have her tested for Gout, for high uric acid. I thought it was water, like the doctor. I thought diuretics were what she needed."

"I've been trying to tell you. We've got to revive her. She was doing so well at the Chinese restaurant only six months ago!"

"Go up for a couple of days. As soon as she is situated at Astrid House. I'll keep you informed by e-mail."

"Thanks. I can fly up this weekend."

"That would probably be best."

"Thank you so much. I love you."

" I love you too. Bye."

Joy went back to her drawing. Slashing and scraping, she threw her whole body, all her energy and emotions into her work. Her Art was her only salvation, the only outlet for her torrent of emotions. The tears she had held back began to flow. Her mother, her backbone, how could she go on without her? She had lost patrons, collectors, friends. In her mid-sixties, it seemed, her world had emptied out of company, people who meant a lot to her. But her mother? No!

Joy ate her bag lunch in gloom. She tasted nothing. Mother! She began to sob. How could she go on?

The phone rang. It was Gary. "Joy, we've moved Amy to Astrid house. She loves it already. She had a good lunch. They did her nails! She played Bingo. Why don't you go up Friday? You're not doing anything. I've e-mailed you flight information. Go up to Reno right away!" It was already Thursday.

"Yes, I have to go. I'll drop everything and go on Friday. It's the only important thing to do right now. Nothing else matters." She hung up the phone, trying to ignore Gary's implication that because she painted all day with little or no demand for her work, she "wasn't doing anything."

Joy drove home feeling a tinge of resentment. After dinner she opened up her Internet and booked a flight on her computer. She would be in Reno tomorrow. She would rent a car and find Astrid House in the mountains. She would be with Amy. Her dad had made it to ninety-four. Perhaps, Amy could revive. She was not yet ninety-one. Living alone was no longer an option for her. Yes, she definitely needed to have full-time help. Yet the idea of Amy needing help to walk appalled her. Until age ninety, she had not been able to keep up with her. Amy walked fast, speeding forward with such determination, it was though she ran General Motors! At age ninety, Amy had slowed just enough so Joy was able to keep up and walk besides her.

Joy had arranged her flight. Everything for the trip would have to go on the credit card. She would figure out a way to pay for it all when she returned.

She really had no choice.

Chapter Twenty-Nine

It all seemed to blur together. The packing, the airport, the flight to Reno, the renting of a car. All that mattered was Amy. Getting to Amy as fast as possible. The doctor had given her the wrong pills. Diuretics were the wrong medication for Amy. She had phoned the doctor months ago. The pills had drained Amy of her water, potassium, sodium, and shot up her uric acid, the opposite of what she needed. Joy had written a letter about gout to her mother and Amy had brought it in to her doctor. Gout was called the "physicians' blind-spot." The doctor had ignored the letter, preferring to keep up the diuretics.

Gary and her mother were in denial about Gout. Joy had suffered two Gout attacks when she had experienced the worst financial pressure. The attacks felt like a combination heart-attack and nervous breakdown.

Doctors, of course, thought they were Gods. Why listen to Amy's daughter? What did she know? She was just an artist!

Her Dad would have made Amy stop the pills. He would have been enraged! Ben had protected Amy from the doctors and their drugs all her life. But unfortunately Ben was no longer around to do this crucial job.

Finally, after two planes, Joy was in the rental car headed for Astrid House. She carefully followed directions after stopping at Whole Foods on Virginia Street and picking up some cherry juice, a natural remedy for high uric acid, along with a pot of red roses. She traveled first north on one freeway, then west on another. Joy found the right off-ramp, but where from there? She guessed it was left. She turned south and found the turn-off for Sunrise and wound around. Where was it? There was a Home Depot. She went right and circled around. She was driving in circles. Stopping, she rechecked the address.

Mother, where are you? She choked back a sob. Finally Joy saw that she could turn left, circling around the store.

Joy followed the road and spotted a large wood-panel structure painted a soft gray. There was a sign on it: "ASTRID HOUSE." It was a large, graceful, contemporary building. She liked it immediately.

She ran in slightly breathless. "I'm Amy's daughter. Where is she?"

"I think she is up in her room, 209."

Circling around, she finally found the elevator. Joy punched the second floor button. Amy was seated in a wheelchair in the hallway. This was shocking enough but watching her mother shake and tremble threw Joy into panic mode.

"Hi Amy."

"Oh, Joy! Gary told me you were…"

Amy was muttering. This wasn't Amy's way. She was always so definite, so decisive, the force of her voice so resounding.

"How are you? Are you ready to go down to dinner?"

"I don't want to live. This is the end."

"Mother, we need you! You can recover. Look at this great place. You can play bridge here; you can have your own room."

"No! I'm through. I'm too weak. I can't even walk."

"Yes, your legs are swollen. But they will go down, your feet too. The doctor gave you the wrong medication.'

"No. I want to go." Suddenly Amy smiled. "Give me my purse."

Joy handed over her mother's beige handbag. At least she had something to share. That might swerve Amy's attitude off this negative mind-set, Joy thought.

With trembling hands, Amy fumbled around in her wallet. She pulled out a photo. It was Joy, age about twenty-one, with a boyfriend and their shaggy sheepdog, Sandy. Amy handed it to Joy with shaking hands.

"Oh! I remember that time so well." Joy was choked with emotion. "You made that outfit for me, didn't you? The soft striped blue-and-white shirt with the large collar, coordinated with a light blue skirt. I remember you sewing it."

Amy nodded.

Joy choked back tears. How could she ever forgive herself for not coming up to Reno sooner? She needed to tell that doctor in no uncertain terms that the pills were to stop! Diuretics had drained Amy and had weakened her to this point where she shook and trembled. They had lowered her zinc and potassium to almost zero. She probably had a Gout attack. Both Gary and Ellie, a neighbor who had been a nurse for forty years, had wanted her to "comply" with the doctors orders and take the diuretics, the harmful "medication." Didn't they monitor her? Couldn't they see this was the wrong thing for Amy? Joy was incensed.

She wheeled Amy down to the elevator and pushed the button. Going through these necessary motions helped ease her despair. This was so unlike Amy, to be dependent. She must be frustrated with her helplessness. That's why she talked this way. Maybe after dinner and a good sleep she would feel differently and be able to live on to celebrate her ninety-first birthday in three months. She wanted Amy to live to see her "come back." Joy wanted to prove she could, once more, be a successful artist. She so wanted Amy to see her successful. Whereas for Joy, what counted was the quality of the work, Amy valued success above all.

"Hello, I hear you flew up from Los Angeles today," the assistant living coordinator smiled. "We will make sure Amy is comfortable here. Everyone loves her already. She played bingo yesterday and got her nails done. She slept very well. In fact, we had to awaken her."

"Yes, this place looks extremely comfortable. I like it so far."

"She can have a mountain-view room. It's on the ground floor. She can move some of her own furniture in and photos. There is a phone-jack for her personal line too."

"I'm sure she'll love it."

"Have a good dinner. I'll show you the room tomorrow morning."

As Joy wheeled Amy to the dining room, an assistant approached them with a pill bottle.

"Amy is to take one a day."

Joy grabbed the bottle. It was the diuretic. "No! Who said she should take this? I told the doctor not to give it to her!"

"We have to follow the doctor's orders. It says right here to give her one before a meal, per day."

"We're going to stop this. I brought her cherry juice. We are going to go holistic for a while."

"O.K. Where is the juice?"

"It's up in her room."

"I'll get it."

Joy breathed a sigh of relief. Gary was wrong, Ellie was wrong, the doctor was wrong. Couldn't they see the degeneration? Couldn't they see how Amy had deteriorated?

The blindness of everyone appalled her. What kind of doctor did Amy have?! She must find a way to terminate this doctor's services and find a holistic doctor for her mother.

In the dining room, Joy found the food to be more than adequate. It was good, the service was fast and attentive. The dinner seemed not to be overly high-fat. There was too much meat, however.

"I shouldn't eat meat, should I?"

"A little, not too much. Here, eat this baked potato." Joy took a spoon and fed Amy. She picked up a napkin and wiped Amy's mouth. This is what Amy had done for her as a baby. Now the reciprocity seemed alien. Amy was now the infant and Joy was the adult. This turnaround seemed bizarre and shocking. Joy tried to keep steady feeding Amy, acting as if the situation was perfectly normal.

"I'd like yogurt for dessert."

"Yes, yogurt will help your digestion. I will ask the waitress."

Amy nodded. She was shaking too hard to hold a spoon. "I shake so much. I sleep so much. It's not possible to go on like this."

"Mother, we need you! You will recover and have a great life here."

"No. I'm through. It's impossible."

Joy ignored this utterance. "This place is wonderful. Look at the mountain view. They're going to move you to your own room with a picture window and some of your own furniture that Grandfather made."

"No, I don't want it. It's time to go."

"You'll make a lot of friends here. Everyone loves you already. They want to have you play bridge with them."

"We need a fourth," a woman in a wheelchair spoke, wheeling herself over to their table. She must have overheard the conversation and was now taking advantage of her knowledge.

"She wants you to play bridge."

"Maybe later. I'm too shaky now."

Francis, who introduced herself, looked at Amy. "You'll be fine. This place is marvelous. Maybe you can play with us tomorrow."

Amy nodded and finished her yogurt. Francis moved her wheelchair back to her table. Joy put her napkin down and got up to wheel Amy back to her room. Amy smiled. "I'm glad you are here. I'm proud of you."

She reached into her purse again, pulling out a hundred-dollar bill. "My friend took me to the bank."

Joy took the crisp bill. How wonderful for Amy to think of her needs! Amy was always generous, always thoughtful, even when she thought she was dying. Joy felt like crying. "Thank you" was all she could say. She felt gratitude mixed with the humiliation of knowing she needed the money.

"I want to go back to bed," Amy said. "I just sleep so much. I have never slept so much! They shook me awake!" She gestured with shaking hands moving rapidly back-and-forth.

Joy wheeled her mother's chair to the bed. With great effort she picked Amy up off the chair, got her high enough to sit and lowered her torso onto the bed. She wheeled the chair away from it and slid Amy's swollen legs and feet onto the comforter. Then she pulled a pillow under her mother's head. She kissed Amy's cheek.

"Good–Bye Amy. Have a sweet nap." Amy fell asleep almost immediately.

Joy left Astrid Houses feeling a depression that was unshakable. Yes, it was true that Amy had lived a long, and, with few exceptions, a healthy life. She did have a hysterectomy and all her teeth pulled, substituting dentures in her middle years. Still, Amy had outlived many of her relatives, her brother and her husband.

The thought of parting with her, however, was inconceivable. Joy felt devastated at the mere thought of doing without her Mother. How could she continue as an artist without the woman who had given her more support than anyone, who encouraged her, who believed in her, who wrote her once a week? Who else could she write to once a week? No, there was no substitute for Amy. No, she couldn't accept this. Amy deteriorated? No, Amy was always the strongest member of the family. She was healthy as an ox—ten oxen! She was the one who made the decisions. Now her decision was to leave. She must respect that decision. *Everyone had the right to make this decision.*

Joy knew this. She repeated this to herself. But convincing her was impossible. She needed her mother. She couldn't accept this giving up.

Driving to the hotel, she found herself weeping. Whatever horrible and traumatic events had happened during her lifetime, nothing compared to this. Nothing could be this bad. Nothing!

She felt like a child again. As a child she had had a nightmare. She had gone with her mother shopping downtown in Chicago, the city where she was born and lived the first six years of her life. They had gone to Marshall Field's, a huge department store. On the escalator she had lost sight of her mother. An empty, lost, and helpless feeling had come over her. *She had lost her mother.* "Mother!" she had cried, waking up. "Mother!"

Now she experienced this same feeling. No, she could not lose her mother. How could she ever bear to lose her mother?

The plane ride home was desolate. Joy had never sunk this low. How could she continue her life as an artist, as hard as it was, without her Mother? Amy was the backbone of her life.

Once home she must attempt dinner. She had a gnawing emptiness in her stomach no food could fill.

Joy was home only one day when Gary called. She had just spent three days in Reno.

"They couldn't wake Amy up. She had a stroke. She was unresponsive. They rushed her back to St. Theresa's hospital. You need to go up again."

"I can leave on Friday. I'll drive this time."

"That would be good. Drive carefully. Do you still have that Power of Attorney?"

"Yes. I have the form."

"We need her to sign it. You should have taken care of that at Astrid House."

"They said I needed two witnesses and they couldn't participate!" Joy moaned.

"Well, we need it. Take it up with you."

"Yes, of course, Will do. Anything else I should do?" Joy asked.

"Find out what medications the doctor is giving her!"

"Yes. They tried to give her yet another diuretic at Astrid House. I stopped them."

"Good work. We're not going to use her present doctor ever again! The doctor at Astrid House agreed with you. She does have Gout."

"I should have gone up to talk to that doctor who prescribed the diuretics, to pin her against the wall! I sent a letter. It wasn't forceful enough."

"The wrong drug has killed many a patient."

"I blame myself for not going up to Reno sooner. I knew it was wrong medication."

"Don't blame yourself. It's not your fault."

"I'll be up there soon again. And I'll bring up the Power of Attorney form."

"Great. I love you."

"I love you too."

On Friday, Joy was back on the road. Her nephew Chris was busy with his music, playing the violin in rehearsal for an upcoming concert. So this trip would be accomplished alone.

She was on the road at six-thirty in the morning. Finally, Gary was seeing the light, admitting that the family had inherited Gout. It had been a tough, long battle. And Amy loved whipped cream! She would pile it on her pie whenever they went to the Peppermill, a huge buffet in a casino where she loved to eat. It was amazing Amy had never had a Gout attack before, as she could not digest fats. People with Gout inherited a missing enzyme so that digesting fats was almost impossible. Instead, swelling of the big- toe, ankles, knees and legs resulted from undigested fatty acids. Amy's ankles were always swollen. She mistakenly attributed this to taking ballet as a child.

As Joy sped along on the highway, going eighty miles an hour, marveling at the pick-up's ability to gather speed and maintain it, she suddenly saw a red light flashing behind her. Uh, oh, she had been caught!

She slowed, coming to a stop finally on the shoulder. A young highway patrol man got out of his patrol-car and sauntered over to her. "You were going eighty in a fifty-five-mile-an-hour speed-limit zone. Let me see your license, registration and insurance."

Joy pulled out her license from her purse and found the registration in the glove compartment, handing them over. The patrolman took them from her.

"How about your insurance?" he questioned, glancing over the cards.

"Officer, I had to drop Hopeford. You see, it's a long story, but they were unfair. Here is proof I had them. I'm in the midst of searching for a new company."

"This is outdated. I will have to cite you for this also. Driving without insurance is a major fine." Grimacing, he walked back to his patrol car and began researching her driving record on his computer.

Finally, after an interminable wait, he came back to the truck. Joy was shaking. She had never gotten a speeding ticket. And she had gone on the Internet looking for a new insurance company, but hadn't time or energy to make a decision. She dreaded what the ticket would amount to. How could she pay it? She was paying dearly for her encounter with this "accident-stager."

"How old are you?" the officer asked.

The question puzzled her. He had her license with her birthdate clearly written on it!

Dumfounded, she answered it honestly. "I just turned sixty-seven."

The officer stared at Joy's face in disbelief. Clearly, he thought she was lying. Yes, women did lie about their age. But they *never* aged themselves! She felt flattered.

"Well, I let you off the insurance ticket. And instead of speeding, I sited you for not wearing your seat belt. I know you were wearing one. It's just that this way the ticket is half-price. Senior discount, you might say!"

"Thank you, officer."

"And get insurance immediately. It's the law. You can't drive without insurance."

"Yes, Sir. I had Hopeford for twenty-seven years. A fellow sideswiped my truck on purpose to collect insurance money. He had his two kids in the back seat. Hopeford awarded him eleven-thousand dollars because I couldn't produce a witness."

"Yes, it's a business. Too bad. But you have to have insurance. Now drive safely." He walked away, leaving a relieved Joy who sat at the wheel stunned, not moving for the next five minutes.

For the rest of the trip, first through the bleached desert, and finally the magnificent snow-blanketed mountains, Joy drove conscientiously, obeying every speed-limit sign. She would have to make a decision about insurance when she returned home. Right this minute, she detested insurance companies.

Joy arrived at St. Theresa's Hospital at five o'clock. She rushed in, ignoring her fatigue, and asked the receptionist where Amy Bravitsky's room was located.

"Room 505," the young, studious-looking woman said. "Take the D elevator to the fifth floor and turn right. It's in the intensive care unit."

She found Amy's bed quickly. Amy was sound asleep, too deeply knocked out to be a natural condition. She suspected Amy had been drugged. Prescription drugs were no better than most street drugs, in her estimation. Her family had always relied on Alternative Medicine, herbs, exercise, rest and vitamin-filled foods.

"Hello Amy," Joy tried in a quiet voice so not to startle her mother awake.

Amy's eyes fluttered open.

"Auf Wiedersehen," she uttered, her German language returning to say farewell.

"Mother, I love you! I'll be here for a few days. You *can* get well!"

A shaky hand waved her away. Once more Amy was deeply asleep.

"Who is the doctor?" Joy demanded, once more out by the reception desk.

"Hello. I'm Doctor Brenner," a young woman nodded. She was brisk and efficient, with an arrogant manner. "Are you her daughter, her Power of Attorney?"

"Yes," Joy answered, though the unfilled form was still in her truck.

"We need you to sign this form for her medications." The Doctor shoved a form towards her. It stated that they could give any drugs they deemed necessary.

"I'm not signing any form until I know what drugs are prescribed."

"We generally do not hand out that information. We're giving her only a few medicines."

"I would like to see it or I will talk to your supervisor."

Reluctantly, the Doctor gave her the list. Joy was shocked to count nine drugs that had been given, almost one per hour, to her mother. On the list was the carcinogenic steroid, Prednizone! Steroids for her petite mother! Did they think she was Arnold Schwarzenegger? They were also giving her the diuretic that had made her mother weakened enough to fall in the first place, as well as aspirin and a blood-thinning sub-stance. Joy knew that aspirin was a blood-thinner, so that drug was redundant.

"Your mother had a stroke, perhaps two strokes. She's very weak."

"She has Gout. This diuretic is what made her ill in the first place. And you don't give a ninety-year-old steroids! I want these eliminated immediately!"

"Steroids need to be tapered off. She can't go off cold-turkey. She'll go wild!"

"No more steroids!"

"She has to take steroids. Her swelling and inflammation are out-of-control."

"No more steroids!"

"We have to use our judgment."

Joy almost shouted, "No more steroids!"

"Raising your voice is not appropriate! It's not appropriate to use this type of tone in a hospital."

"You aren't listening to me. We will eliminate all but two of these drugs."

"Yes, we will. But yelling is not appropriate."

"Do you believe that giving a ninety-year-old woman two CAT-scans in a row and nine prescription drugs, almost one-per-hour, *is* appropriate?"

"We do our best."

"Well, it's not good enough. You doctors have been turned into drug dealers!"

"We do what we think is appropriate."

Joy almost laughed bitterly at this snotty doctor's limited vocabulary. She felt like slapping her face. "I'll see you tomorrow" was all Joy said and turned to go.

Drug companies, like insurance companies, were a business.

Chapter Thirty

Gaude Velasquez sat in an armchair in an empty house, his foot raised high on its footstool, propped up even higher with a stack of pillows. It was still bandaged and swollen. He walked with crutches which were now leaning against the arm of the chair. The silence reverberated against the empty walls. His thoughts were empty too. All he felt was rage. The need for vengeance was uppermost in his mind.

He had spent three months in the downtown Men's Correctional Institution, three tortuous, horrible months. He had lived with murderers, dope dealers, addicts, rapists and thieves. His dignity had been abolished in this sordid environment. All his self-respect had drained down the tubes; he felt his life was at rock-bottom. After he had served the three months, Mel Grant was able to spring him. After all, the only crime they had been able to pin on him was bruising Martha Taylor's wrist and resisting an officer. Accident- staging had not been proved. He had been found "not guilty" by Hopeford Insurance Company and been awarded monetarily. So they couldn't pin that on him, thank God.

But what good was the money now? Maria was in Mexico City with Jorge, Juanita and Juan. And they were not coming back. He missed them with a raw ache that no salve assuaged. He had tried calling Maria at her parents' home but his wife had hung up on him. She had made it perfectly clear that she wanted nothing more to do with him.

He sighed, got up, and, hopping on one foot, grabbed the crutches. He hobbled to the kitchen and got the coffee-maker started. He had to make a plan. That plan had to eradicate Joy Bravitsky. She had made all this trouble for him, had caused him so much pain and suffering. It was her fault he had to spend time in jail. It was her fault he was now disabled, unable to walk without crutches. The more he thought about it, the angrier he became.

Gus had gotten the news in prison. Shortie went to court and the trial had found him guilty of Involuntary Manslaughter. The judge had given him "twenty-years-to-life." He had been sent to another prison upstate, in Chico. Perhaps, when some time had elapsed, he could visit Tomaso. Then again, Shortie might never want to see him. He would like to call Rosie, Shortie's wife. But probably Rosie would hang up on him too. Well, Shortie chose to participate in accident-staging, after all. It was his choice. Gaude hadn't forced him into it. Velasquez had merely taught him a few tricks, a few ins and outs of the "trade."

And Shortie hadn't listened to him about the dangers of left-turn strikes. It was Shortie's fault. Gaude felt no guilt, whatsoever. Nevertheless, he felt ostracized. The house was way too empty. The silence seemed to mock him.

He made his way back to his chair without his coffee-cup. He just couldn't carry much of anything that couldn't fit under his arm. Dr. Schuster said he would be like this for at least three more months. It would be over six months that he would endure incapacitation. Half a year down the drain!

The more he thought about it, the angrier Gus became. Joy Bravitsky. *It was all her fault.*

He wished he had never met up with her. He must eliminate her from the planet!

Velasquez knew where she lived. He knew where she worked. An artist! It's too bad she would never have another show. He would see to that shortly. He must get a clear head, must figure it out. He needed money. He would hit her again, as crazy as this seemed, this time making sure she was terminally injured. He would make some money, thereby killing two birds with one stone!

The phone rang. Gaude limped over to the desk.

"Mel Grant on the line. Is this Gaude Velasquez?" the receptionist asked.

"Yes, put him on."

"Hello Gus. How are you today?"

"Miserable. Glad you asked."

"Sit down. Maria wants a divorce."

"She what?"

"She sent me the papers via her attorney in Mexico."

"Tell her to go to Hell!"

"Listen, we have to follow through. It's not up to you."

"Oh God! What more can go wrong?"

"It's not the end of the world. You can recover and start a new family."

"So easy."

"Yes, and you can have visitation rights for the kids."

"I would like to see them, yes."

"You're going to have to support them, of course. And you need money for this divorce action."

"And where am I going to get that? All I have now is some small disability checks."

"When you get well, you can find a job."

"Glad you think I would lower myself to work for someone else."

"Sometimes we have to make sacrifices."

"I've made them! Look at me. I'm a wreck!"

"You'll recover. In the meantime, I need you to sign some papers. Can you come into the office?"

"Are you kidding? I can't drive. And the chauffeur has the day off!"

Mel laughed. "At least you haven't lost your sense of humor! I'll come over to you later today. How about five o'clock?"

"Sure, maybe we can grab a taco in the neighborhood."

"Fine. See you then."

Gus hung up. He thought of Maria and his children. A divorce! How could he survive it? He was a wreck. His life was ruined. He couldn't even walk! He thought again of Joy Bravitsky, his face growing red with rage. All he had done to her was scratch her truck's front bumper! And look what she had done to him! Enraged, he picked up a ceramic jar and threw it against the wall where it smashed into hundreds of tiny pieces.

Velasquez knew he would get her. He would smash her to bits!

At precisely five o'clock there was a knock on the door. Gus fumbled for his crutches, catching one as it started to topple. He clumsily got up, adjusted the supports, and hopped his way to the door. He felt like a rabbit.

He opened the door to Mel Grant. Mel was overweight, short and stocky. His belly hung enormously over his belt. He had dyed black hair, greased and combed forward over his large bald spot. Black sunglasses with gold trim hid his beady brown eyes. He was dressed in an oversized black suit with enormous shoulder pads, a crisp white shirt and maroon polka-dot tie with an elaborate gold clasp. A Rolex watch adorned his wrist.

"Hello Mel. You're right on time to catch this train-wreck!"

"Sit down, Gus. Try to stay off that foot for a while longer."

"Yea, it's not healed yet. The doctor said six agonizing months."

"So you'll be able to walk normally again in three months, having served the prior three months in jail."

"Yeah, in the pen! I'll be able to walk normally as an ex-jail-bird. God, I hope so! I can't stand this stumbling around much longer."

Gus noticed Mel's hair. Some gray streaks were beginning to show through the slicked, dark comb-over. But he was sharp as ever.

"Listen Gus, accident-staging is not all it's cracked up to be. I'll support you and be on your side whatever you do. But isn't it time to rethink your career?"

"I don't know, Mel. I'm good at what I do. Look at all the money we made! A couple of minutes equaled eleven-thousand dollars. That's five-thousand-five-hundred dollars a minute! How else can I make that kind of money?"

"Well, maybe if you were Cary Grant."

"Wrong time frame. Maybe, Brad Pitt!"

Mel laughed ruefully. "Yes you made big bucks, but you have to factor in what you lost. You lost your health, your wife, your kids. You lost your ability to walk normally for six months."

"It's the fault of that bitch Bravitsky! Any normal victim would not have given me any trouble."

"She's anything but normal. You picked a doozy!"

"She didn't look it. A bum in painted-up clothes that looked like thrift-shop apparel. Skinny, old bag! Nervous and shaking."

"I'll say this in her favor. She has a college degree. I looked it up."

"No one outthinks me. I don't care if she has a Ph.D. from Yale. Is she famous?"

"She has had some shows and reviews. She has some notoriety."

"She's not Picasso!"

"She's a woman."

"Look Mel. Let's get at the truth. I barely grazed her bumper. Maybe she had a little pain for a month. In return, I lost my wife, my kids, my freedom, my health and my ability to walk. How fair is that?"

"Life isn't fair. Speaking of fair, I need you to counter-sue your wife for divorce."

"I don't want a divorce."

"It's too late. Maria wants one. In California, only one partner needs to file for a divorce. If you counter-sue, you can say she was a negligent mother. Maybe save yourself some dough."

"Oh, God! She did as good a job as she could. How can I pin negligence on her?"

"Look, just sign these papers. I'll take care of the details."

"O.K. You got me out of jail." He took the pen Mel proffered.

"Listen. I'm going to give you good advice once more. Then I'm going to drop the subject once and for all. *Drop accident-staging as a career!*"

Gus was silent. He dropped his head as if he were praying to God. The room reverberated with silence. Somewhere a dog barked, a bird sang, a cat meowed. The fading sun threw its last rays on the sidewalks. Life went on unabated outside the small house. Inside, it was as if life had screeched to a halt.

Finally, a noise was heard from Gus. It was a sob, starting from deep within his chest. It startled Mel with its intestinal bellow, as if all his organs were crying out in pain.

Mel waited. Gus's tears flowed out as he cried in spurts, trying to breathe between sobs. His chest heaved, as if he was trying to throw his distraught condition out of his body.

"It was…"

Mel waited.

"It was not what I…"

"What did you want?" Mel prodded.

"I planned to be an attorney like you." Gus finally was composing himself enough to get one sentence out. He caught his breath that came in irregular spurts.

"Well, it's not too late. You can finish your law degree. Take the bar. Start over. Be an upstanding citizen. It's not a bad life, pays well, *is* respected. And you can legally make money cheating people!"

Gus tried to laugh. He felt only pain and the hurt of an unused conscience. "I guess you're right." He wiped the tears from his face with the sleeve of his shirt.

"I'm glad you're seeing the light. You have talent and wits. Crime might pay for a while. But the losses catch up with you. You met the wrong victim this time; next time they might kill you."

"You're right. I need to get hold of myself. I don't know how I got so desperate. Just one more strike. I have to kill Joy Bravitsky!"

"Gus, I'm warning you. Stay away from that broad!"

"We'll see. She's got to pay for this."

Mel grimaced. He thought when Gus broke down he had finally seen the light. Now he doubted Gus had seen anything. He sighed, shrugging his shoulders.

"O.K. How about that taco now?" Gus gestured towards the door.

Gaude grabbed his crutches. Hobbling, with Mel's help, he waited for his attorney to open the door.

Together this unlikely pair, one stout and healthy, the other tall, thin and crippled, went out to face the dying sun in search of a Mexican restaurant.

Chapter Thirty-One

"What's happening with your mom?" Carey asked.

"She's not doing well. She keeps insisting this is the end. Mostly she sleeps. I can't face life without her. She was the only one who consistently believed in me."

"We believe in you."

"Thank you. But nothing can replace the support you receive from your mother. Gary is going up next. The doctor agrees this may be the end. I really can't face it. It's so hard!"

"You went up two weekends in a row. It's Gary's turn."

"My nephew Chris went up last weekend with his girlfriend Alice. They moved Amy to Covenant Convalescent Home on Shelter Lane. He didn't like the place at all. He fed Amy and got her clothes from the house. Astrid House transferred her clothes too but they couldn't remember or find them. They are seriously overworked there. And the place is dark, depressing and stinks. I wish she would get well enough to go back to Astrid House. Convalescent homes are not the place to pass away. My dad died there. But Amy is stable. Our hopes are that she will get well enough to go back to Astrid House so we can celebrate her ninety-first birthday there."

"I'll pray for her! Who is Cameron's girlfriend? What is she like?"

"She's really wonderful. She studied Art at the Rhode Island School of Design, very prestigious. Now she's a curator at MOCA. She's an elegant, small-boned brunette, unpretentious. Very mature and knowledgeable for her age. She's only twenty-four."

"Wow! He has good taste! By the way, Stan has started shooting *Mixed Messages*. He's on location today, filming in Altadena. It's at the corner of Sierra View Drive and Foothill Boulevard."

"Oh, that's right near me. It would be a privilege to watch him in action. Can I visit the set? I wouldn't go really close but watch from a distance."

"I think it might be alright. I don't know. They're very strict about viewers on the set. But people do watch from afar. I think that would be fine."

"Great. I'll go at lunch time."

"Bye. And if you write or talk to your Mother today, give her my best."

"Thanks, I will."

Joy hung up and went back to work on her study. She was doing an oil on paper, a study for *Earthpeace,* a large canvas seven-foot square. It would have joyous colors: yellow, yellow-orange, turquoise, blue and deep rose-red. Her new canvases were a celebration of life and a prayer for peace. Her collector, Bill Roman, had always admired her "spiritual strength," an over-riding force cohering the amalgamation of energy and colors she threw into her paintings. Roman had been a patron and had paid her monthly for two years against the canvases he would acquire. He had become a friend and visited her studio once a week in order that he "wouldn't miss something." When he died in 1995 at age eighty-five, she was bereft. All the color suddenly disappeared from her work. She worked on in grief, using only black-and-white for months, dedicating most of her drawings and paintings to him.

Now she was excited to see Stan Moshan in motion. She would clean up at eleven-thirty and drive to Altadena and have lunch nearby. The clock moved rapidly when she was engrossed in her work. Focus made her oblivious. She was surprised to see it was almost twelve when she put her brushes down.

Rapidly, she cleaned the brushes and put them in a large blue ceramic jar another artist had given her for brushes. They made a display like a floral arrangement, neatly fanning out. Joy changed to a clean tunic she had brought with her that morning to cover her jeans, and put on clean shoes. Soon she was in her truck headed for Altadena, a small town just north of Pasadena.

The production company had quit for lunch, Joy saw, as soon as she arrived. She didn't ask where they had gone, but merely spied a fast-food stand where she could order a sandwich. She found a table near the set and ate the egg salad on rye with pickles and mustard, drinking water from the big bottle she had brought along. Acting was an art that mesmerized her.

Joy was a silent actress when she performed in front of the canvas. The results were shown later. Acting had to be done in front of cameras or a live audience. She appreciated the guts it took to perform while being watched. Perhaps that was why Joy had picked visual arts; she could create in the privacy of her studio. The shows would happen later when no one could see her secrets, or mistakes, or what she threw away or painted over.

At one o'clock on the dot, the actors moved to the top of the hill where they would enact the scene scheduled for that day. Stan marched onto the hill in a Navy blue Armani suit. In front of him was a shiny red sports car. He looked statuesque and handsome. He began to move about the scene as the cameras began to roll. Joy wanted a closer look and spied a vacant spot nearer the action. It would afford a better view than where the small crowd gathered at the bottom of the hill.

She had just reached the spot which offered a much better vantage point, when a man in a uniform walked abruptly up to her. "Let me see your driver's license," he demanded.

"Why?" Joy asked stupefied. She wasn't driving.

"Just show me. You're on private property. We rented this land for the shoot."

Joy complied, pulling out her license from her purse and handed it to him.

"Do you know someone?" he asked.

"Yes, I know Stan Moshan. He's a friend."

"Well, you have to move down the hill where that crowd is. We can't have anyone on the set."

"Sure, I understand. I'm sorry if I got too close." Joy took her license back and headed down the hill to where she had started out.

There seemed to be a lot of buzzing going on among the security staff. It seemed that they didn't believe her and were trying to decide something. Suddenly, the man in uniform put his hand in his mouth and gave a shrill whistle. A group of white-clad figures careened down the hill like a flock of seagulls, toward Joy. All the action stopped abruptly on the set. Stan stood motionless, glaring down into the crowd.

"Oh God, I didn't want to disrupt the film," Joy winced. The white figures were rapidly besides her led by the uniformed man. "You lied. You don't know anyone here," he said. "Where's your car?"

"My truck is over there," Joy pointed. "I'm sorry, I didn't mean to disrupt the filming. I thought…"

Two of the white-clad figures approached her on either side, grasping each of her arms and led her to her truck as if she were a criminal.

"I will go on my own," she declared hotly, shoving the security-guards off. "You are a liar," one of them repeated.

"Don't come back!" another one of them said as they approached her truck.

"I won't!" She snapped, pushing the electronic door opener on her key chain.

Joy drove off in a huff, the blood wildly pulsing in her veins. She certainly did not like being called a liar! And all those security guards! She could only feel guilt, however, for disrupting Stan's movie. Would he ever forgive her?

Back at the studio, Joy tried to calm her nerves. It was impossible for her to continue her work. What had she accomplished? *That was a really bad idea.* Stan was a friend, and now he probably wouldn't speak to her! This is how she valued her friendships?

Her mind worked in circles over and over, trying to come to some rationalization about what she had done. Of course, they were a bit paranoid. But she really hadn't been that close. The spot she had chosen had a good view, but wasn't in anyone's way. Why had they attacked her as if she were a terrorist? She wasn't Bin Laden, for God's sake.

The clock ticked ahead, but it remained useless to try to accomplish anything. Her mind just went around in vicious circles. She felt like a criminal caught in the act.

Finally, at four-thirty, the phone rang. It was Stan.

"I didn't know you were coming to the set today. I'm sorry about what happened."

"No, it's my fault. I interrupted your scene. I really feel bad about this."

"Don't worry. I explained to the security staff that I know you, but it was too late. You were already gone. John got your name wrong. He said you were Jody, not Joy. This won't happen again. But be sure to tell me when you want to come to a set. They were just doing their job. We don't tolerate surprise visits for a reason."

"I'm really sorry. It won't happen again." Joy felt like groveling at his feet. How could she have been so foolish and thoughtless?

"Forget it. Just get back to your work. I'll see you soon."

Maybe Stan would forgive her someday. She felt like a dunce. Humiliation had a sting that didn't evaporate quickly, like a drop of rain on the sidewalk would. She had felt about twelve years old when they had escorted her to her truck.

She called Carey.

"Hi, what's up?" her friend said.

"Carey, I want to deeply apologize. I went to the set to surprise Stan. But the security guards flew down on me and I got my comeuppance."

Carey laughed. "Don't worry about it. Stan is used to interruptions. He'll forget this in a New York minute."

"I won't *ever* forget it! I felt like a clown or a convicted felon."

"He'll laugh about it tomorrow. We both love you; don't worry another second about this. It's just a glitch in the CD. Worry about your mother. That's worth worrying about."

"Yes. I talked to her today. She said almost one sentence. Then some babbling. The rest was breathing, or trying to. She had a Gout attack and a stroke! She has to learn to speak all over again. They're giving her a speech therapist. I'm just worried about her constantly. My niece Bridget has her new baby, Audrey, and is pre-occupied breast-feeding and adjusting to her schedule. I want her to go to Reno. This might be the last chance for Amy to see her great-grand-daughter. I feel paralyzed by this. I write postcards to Amy everyday. The social worker says her room is decorated with them."

"I suppose Bridget is waiting for July, for Amy's ninety-first birthday. That's only three months away."

"Yes, I pray that she'll make it to celebrate and my mom will be able to meet Audrey. I urge Amy everyday. *Mother has stopped telling me that she doesn't want to live, however.* So there is hope."

"That's good. I hope she recovers. Stan definitely forgives you for coming to the set. I'll remind him to call you."

"He already called and said to forget about it. The security-guard said my name was Jody which caused the mix-up. I really appreciate your tolerance of my craziness!"

"Thanks, I appreciate your tolerance of my craziness!"

Carey laughed, "Bye for now."

The next day Joy received a blank fax. This was one of Stan's many ways of "communicating." Or of making her laugh out loud.

All was as usual with Stan at least. If only the situation was as easy with her mother.

Chapter Thirty-Two

"**W**e're engaged!" Chris was jubilant. "I asked Alice to marry me and she said "Yes!" Joy and Chris were walking from the studio to the Thai restaurant down the street.

"Congratulations! Did you give her a ring?"

"Yes, I found a stunner at a vintage jewelry store."

"When's the wedding?"

"I don't know. We're moving to New York City at the end of the summer."

"Oh! I know you've always wanted to live there. But it seems you have established important roots in Los Angeles: you play the violin in the Pasadena Symphony and Alice landed that great job as a MOCA curator! You'll have to start all over in New York."

"We don't like it here. We gravitate to the people in New York."

"You'll have to sell your car. You don't need a car in Manhatten."

Chris looked dubious for a second. He hadn't considered what he was giving up.

"What are you going to do there? You won't drop your music!" She was worried. Of course New York loved artists, musicians and entertainers. However the hard life was not conducive to growth for the artist. California was less demanding monetarily, and more open to creative living. There was more solitude for invention. The sunny climate was more laid back and casual, more conducive to innovation and discovery. New York was crazy, fun and intellectually stimulating but there were so many distractions in the Big Apple. Joy was not sure she would get any work done if she had set up a studio there.

"I'm going to teach math."

"Are you applying for a degree in education?"

"There's a college there that I've applied to. It's a two-year program."

"What about Alice? She has such a tremendous position here working for MOCA."

"She's looking at non-profits. She already has leads."

They had reached the Thai restaurant. The day was overcast, mirroring Joy's feelings. She had lost her father two years ago, at age ninety-four. Now she might lose her mother. On top of that, she was soon to lose the companionship of Chris and Alice.

Joy had taken Alice to the Norton Simon Museum after brunch one Sunday, before Chris's concert. Alice had proven to be both knowledgeable and inquisitive while gazing at the Van Gogh's and Cezanne's. Joy had enjoyed looking at the Masters with Alice and had invited her to come back again to see more of the museum. Chris was playing Bach, so they only skimmed the dense collection, passing too quickly over the Rembrandts and Picassos. Downstairs the Simon had a special exhibition of Color-Field painters they hadn't had time to get around to, though Joy had gone once before to view the Nolands, Frankenthalers, Olitskis, Poons, and Stellas with their bold, bright color and effortless, flawless fields of color. To make an effortless-looking painting took years of practice. To make clean fields of color as opposed to mud took discipline and skill. "That looks easy," or "My child could have done that" was, ironically, a great compliment.

Joy was overjoyed to have a new art-friend who now would be a family member.

Wasn't there some law against losing too many of your close family and friends all at once? She tried to smile and converse as usual with Chris who was enthusiastic and hopeful, full of schemes and plans. But now she was silent. Grief was what she felt.

"Worried about your mother?" Chris noticed she wasn't talking.

"Yes. I think about her every day. I send postcards and call. But now I'm a little sad about losing you too because you're moving."

"We might be back. Maybe five years will be enough."

"Just don't forget you're an artist!"

Chris looked sad then. He wanted New York to offer its advantages without giving up the toehold he and Alice had already made in L.A. But, unfortunately, no one can have everything. Would Chris and Alice become just another ordinary couple? These two were talented, with lives in the Arts Community. Of course, they could pursue their music and Art careers in New York. But it would be harder. All the competition from Art careerists packed together like sardines vying for the same galleries, museums and orchestras. And the battle with the harsh weather, high overhead, and all that cement!

"Knightly Gallery wanted me to move to New York back in the seventies. I didn't want to move. My inspiration is California. When I am in New York, I wear gray clothes."

"There *is* a lot of cement there. We're thinking of living in Brooklyn. It's five minutes away from the city." Chris still sounded excited.

Joy and her nephew entered the restaurant and were seated at the outside patio. "It's not too cold for you?" Chris asked after they were given menus.

"It is gloomy today!" Joy tried to feel upbeat about Chris's news. But she was beginning to wonder about her lonely life, soon to get lonelier. She had stuck it out for forty years on Old York. Despite the almost five-hundred collectors she had amassed over the years, Joy had only sold one work so far since January and that was to her nouveau-riche cousin in Atlanta, Georgia. The year was the bleak-est she had ever seen.

Yet Joy had grown to love California and could not conceive of painting without its constant input of gorgeous colors, shapes and movement. No gallery in sight. Joy wondered if she should move too. Once she had been fortunate to have the best of both worlds—the easy living in California and shows in New York where the world- marketplace for art was still centered.

"What are you thinking about?" Chris wondered at her silence, so different from Joy's characteristic effervescence.

"I just was wondering about my life. I chose a lonely path, all artists do. But it seems to get unbearably lonely as I get older. So many of my friends and collectors have died. Some moved away. I'm so happy for you and Alice. But I'll really miss you too."

"We'll definitely miss you. But we love New York. We'll be start-ing our life together in a place we love to visit."

"Yes, visiting New York is one thing. Living there is another. You don't know how good you have it here."

"You're probably right. But we've made the decision. And we're excited about it!"

"I remember many artists friends of mine who moved to New York to 'make it' as an artist. They got really mad when I was the one who got the show on Madison Avenue without moving a step."

Chris laughed. "So what's new in your life?"

"I'm getting an intern next week, also from the Rhode Island School of Design, the school Alice attended. Leah is the daughter of Theresa, my friend from the Y that you met at the impromptu birthday party I had before the MOCA auction last year. Remember, we all viewed my *Earthslide* drawing at the Geffen before you steered us to that Japanese sushi place nearby?"

"Yes. Lucky you! You can give her all the scut-work you give assistants, like when I worked for you a few times."

"I admit it's mostly stretching, sizing and priming canvases, mopping the floor, unclogging the sink, killing black-widow spi-ders, escorting lizards out of the studio and other glamorous jobs!"

"But she'll learn a great deal about what it's like to be a full-time artist," Chris observed. "Most of it is just plain, hard slave-work. That should dispel any notions she might have of glamour!"

"I'll let you know how she does. What do you plan to do with your summer?"

"Get ready to leave L. A."

"You'll go to Reno for Amy's ninety-first birthday party if she makes it?"

"Of course. Gary, my Dad, says the goal is for her to walk into P.F. Chang's on her own without help. It's almost unbelievable a whole year has almost passed.

"Yes! The year flew by. Dad and I plan to get her back to the airy Astrid House instead of that dark convalescent home she's wallowing in."

"I really hope she makes it. She wasn't in good shape when I went up with Alice."

"Where did you propose to Alice?"

"Just off Highway 395 before Mono Lake."

"Did you get on your knee?"

"Sure did!"

"She told me she really loves you. She said she can't picture her life without you."

"She told you that?" Chris blushed. "I feel the same. I love her very much."

Joy and Chris finished their lunch and paid, going Dutch. Walking back to the studio, Joy and Chris were silent. Joy was trying to digest what her life would be like without the closeness of her family. But it was impossible. She wanted desperately to talk Chris out of his plans to move. But that wouldn't be right. Chris had his life ahead of him. He had just turned thirty-one. He would have his adventure in New York as a newlywed. He had always voiced the desire to live in New York, as long as she had known him. If the cost of living and the climate didn't kill him, not to mention giving up the Pasadena Symphony, while Alice gave up MOCA… Perhaps he would find excitement as a math teacher.

Still, Joy doubted that he would find it as rewarding as someone who didn't have his musical gifts and eye for painting. But it was his decision. She must not meddle, pry or argue. She would visit them in New York and find out the story soon enough. They had to find out for themselves. Perhaps they would love it. Who was she to predict anything?

"Well, I'll be going," Chris said after they had reached the studio. He gave her a hug. His sad look as he departed confirmed his love.

Joy sighed. She loved to visit New York. It was an exciting city. But after a week or ten days, she was itching to come back to L. A. to work quietly in her sky-lit space.

The next day Leah came in to work at Joy's studio. She was a short red-head, good-looking and energetic. Joy had begun working with aluminum stretcher bars and had gotten one for Leah to stretch, size and prime a canvas, to teach her the trade. Interns worked for credit rather than cash, a boon at this point, the slowest year ever. The economy was dragging its feet. Artists that had galleries and shows were selling one piece or nothing, even with reviews. One of her friends even got a review in *Art Forum* magazine but she had only sold one painting in a show of at least thirty works. Another had gotten a review in the *L. A. Times* newspaper, but he had sold nothing. So an intern was invaluable.

"Welcome. So you want to learn how to be an Artist?"

'Yes. I'm especially interested in a green environment."

"Everything I use is fume-free. It took two years of experimentation and research to find what I could use. I got totally sick from acrylic fumes when I was using big drums of Rhoplex for commissions like four ten-foot paintings for the Bonaventure Hotel and the *Black Forest* Series."

"What do you use now?"

"I use oils, getting cold-pressed linseed oil from a manufacturer in Canada. And the thinner I use, suggested by Brice Marden, is Orange Terpenes from a perfume company! It's made from orange rinds. Do you smell anything?"

"No! It's miraculous. At Rhode Island School of Design, they installed a complicated ventilation system in the painting department. Still, they told us that we could only paint for one hour a day."

"You're kidding! What can you ever accomplish in one hour?"

"Nothing much. Plus they want us to think of technology, the Internet and paint three-to-five paintings a week about that!"

"Oh my God! No wonder you were complaining. Theresa said you weren't happy in the painting class."

"How do *you* make the stretcher-bars? We just went to the Art supply store and got sticks that you slide together. They are wobbly."

"We made them from scratch for forty years. Now I get them from a factory in Gardena that makes aluminum stretcher bars that I like a lot. You have to learn to work with them, but once I figured out the differences, they're wonderful. Light and strong and perfectly square. With wood, it's hard to get them perfect, and they do change with the weather or damage from shipping."

"You made stretcher-bars from scratch!? Wow!"

"It's not that hard. I usually had an assistant to help. I have a table-saw and clamps. That's really all you need besides lumber, nails and a hammer."

"My paintings on the store-bought, wobbly bars get crooked fast. My mother has one that is cataclysmic!'

Joy laughed. "Here is the roll of canvas. I use number ten cotton-duck. Number twelve is too thin. I never get canvases pre-stretched as they mostly use the thinner weight which is less expensive. This roll has fifty yards and it takes two people to roll and unroll it. I buy one hundred yards at a time and the supplier re-rolls it into two cylinders for easier transport."

Together they unrolled the canvas, crouching down on the floor, using all their weight and strength, then set the five-foot stretcher-bar on the piece. Joy showed Leah how to measure four inches all around for the tacking, then cut with scissors, first making a slit, then sliding the scissors through the canvas, tearing it evenly. Next she taught Leah how to staple it to the wood-strip backing, using one staple at the center of each side, then one on either side of that, continuing, circling around, until the corners.

"This way it stretches evenly," she explained. "Stop when you get to the corners and I will show you how to do them."

"I've never gotten the corners right. And no one has been able to show me how to do it."

Joy went back to her study, an oil on paper that might become a sort of map for a canvas. Not all oils on paper were studies; some she did just for itself. Meanwhile, Leah worked quietly at the back of the studio. It was nice to have companionship, a worker to take some of the loneliness out of the place. And it made it seem more like a functioning studio. Leah was to answer the phone saying, "Joy Bravitski's Studio." She felt fortunate to have an assistant again. It made more of a productive milieu and at least felt like a successful, working studio, even though practically nothing was happening at the moment.

However, talking with Leah, she suddenly saw the time-warp she was painting in. It came to her like a revelation, or rather like a slap-in-the-face. Joy spent months on a lyrical abstraction with hints of landscape, reveling in color, shape, line and contrast while Leah was instructed to think of cold technology, whipping out canvases on teetering, flimsy, cheap stretchers. Joy painstakingly prepared the canvas, sizing and priming. The stretcher bars were either sturdily built with the help of an assistant, or factory- built of aluminum. Joy often executed five or more studies before she was satisfied to start her painting. She saw in a flash how old-fashioned and out-of-date she must look to the young gallery owners, at least ten of whom had rejected her work. They wanted "Conceptual Art," something more like Leah was describing.

"I guess if I did a pile of tires on the floor, I would be more acceptable now," Joy noted.

Leah laughed. "Or a pile of trash. I saw something like that in a museum."

"Notice the contrast between the puffed up tires and the flat ones. Note how the artist utilized this to his advantage, to reference contemporary life."

Marcel Duchamp had been pulverized for so long, it was no longer off-putting or ostentatious to nail a twig to the wall or put four bricks on the floor and call it art. He was the first "conceptual artist," putting a urinal on a museum wall. By this brazen act, he thumbed his nose at the art world, making it all one big joke.

"Oh, it's Art!" Joy was screaming with laughter now. But underneath was pain. The pain of showing her work to young gallery dealers and drawing a blank from them. The pain of constant rejection. Of course they wouldn't "get it." And how many of the dealers, young or old, had ever even taken an art history class?

It seemed as if anything was art. And the less like art it was, the more it was considered Art! Joy could only scratch her head dubiously. This revelation was one she had never faced. Now it was revealed starkly by Leah's observations. Dealers who wanted trendy work when "conceptual art" was "in" would not relate to honest painting.

"Or if it looks like an already accepted artist's work. An artist who battled it out to do original art and was, at first, rejected. I've listened to a dealer tell me their hot, new young artist's work looks 'just like Picasso!'"

Leah laughed again. She had now stretched the canvas and was applying the sizing: hot glue, scrubbing it deep into the fibers with a small scrub brush. Joy enjoyed showing Leah how to make art that would last. Her paintings would not deteriorate over time due to shoddy workmanship. Her paintings dating back forty years still looked fresh. "I'm old fashioned, I guess. I'm teaching you to make Art that is thoughtful, time-consuming, and made with classical, time-proven techniques."

Theresa, Leah's mother would tell Joy a few days later that what Leah was learning from Joy was "nothing like she had been taught in school." She'd added that Leah had become sore from all the stretching and bending.

Besides preparing a canvas, she had asked Leah to remove large paintings from storage for inventory. Leah would unwrap them and hang them up. Joy would ask Leah for her opinion. The painting was judged "hit-or-miss" and either digitally photographed or was taken down, staples removed, canvas cut up and then the pieces thrown out. Yes, it was cruel to edit one's work. And it was labor-intensive.

"Remember what Matisse said," Joy told Leah. "A bad painting sent out is the artist's worst enemy."

Leah agreed. "I'm here to learn. This seems like the way to paint."

They worked together in silence for a while. Then Leah asked, "Do you have a website?"

"You know, I really need one, Joy replied. " I've been thinking about it."

"I think your work would shine in New York. Lyrical painting has not died there like it has in L.A."

"You're probably right. It's a good suggestion. I'll look into it."

"I can help you build one with these photos you're taking. Our generation is tech-savvy. We're tied to our computers and cell phones, I-phones and tablets. Let's start it while I'm here to help you."

"You're right. A website might even help get my work back in New York where it's appreciated. The young Culver City galleries here, where I'd like to show, don't get it. And it seems L.A. just isn't into lyrical color-painting. Times have changed. I'm not thinking of technology when I paint. I'm thinking of sky, trees, lakes, the ocean, freeways, speed, aerial views when you fly over, or drive past lush country. When you move past landscape, it becomes a blur. I use shape and colors that blend together, reflecting that indistinct-ness. I'm an abstract landscape painter."

"There are websites that have software to create a do-it-yourself website, like Wix. All you do is plug in your photos and information."

"That sounds simple until I try to do it."

"I'm here to help."

"O.K. How do we start?"

"You have a computer?'

"Yes. I'll bring it down here."

The next day Joy brought her laptop to the studio. Before Leah had finished her internship, they had created JoyBravitskiArt.com together. There were several categories: paintings, drawings, panel drawings, oil on paper, and her page from *L.A. Rising*. A short biography was included. The home page featured a photo of Joy against an eight-foot painting in blue sea colors.

"We made a website!" Joy told Carey excitedly. "Leah is a tech-pro!"

"I'll tell Stan. He knows a few galleries in New York. I told him what Leah said about your work, that it would be appreciated in New York. He said he would recommend you. He can tell them about your website. I'll check it out first."

"You said you two wanted to look at new paintings?"

"Yes, we were to come by last Thursday, but Stan is still filming. This Saturday would be better. Meanwhile, we'll check out your site."

"That would be wonderful. Stan's recommendation would carry a lot of weight."

"He does collect. He patronizes Stuckup Gallery uptown."

"I've heard of Stuckup. But aren't they awfully snobby?"

"Depends on who you are."

"I'm just an artist. I guess they would be kinder to collectors who spend money?"

"Yes, and Stan loves art. As you know he collects when he has film work."

"What time do you want to come by on Saturday?"

"Probably in the afternoon. I'll ask Stan, but tentatively two o'clock would be fine. I'll call you tomorrow."

On Saturday afternoon Carey and Stan came to the studio. "Your work is getting better and better," Stan commented as he looked around. His eyes darted from one large canvas to the next, drinking in the color and gesture. He seemed to dance as he went from painting to painting. *It was as if he absorbed the gestures in the paintings bodily and mimicked them.* "What's this one called?" he asked stopping in front of her very latest painting.

"It's called *Flame Pond* (for Japan). The dark red elongated oval is the radiation pond. It's radio-active!"

Stan laughed. "How much you want for it?"

"My large canvases were ten thousand for many years. Let's say fifteen thousand."

"That's too low. How about I give you twenty-five thousand? I consider it a rock-bottom bargain price."

"It's too much money! Galleries take fifty percent. If I take that much from you, a gallery would have to charge fifty thousand!"

"Well, galleries will come again. But for now, I like that painting. I'll write you a check and send it tomorrow."

"I'll send you a receipt." Joy was ecstatic. "Where should I deliver it?"

"Carey and I are buying a new home. The wedding is July. We should have a new address by then. Does the painting fit in your truck?"

"My new truck, yes. I can get six-feet-by-four stretchers or canvases easily in the truck bed."

" Great! Can't wait to have it! Meanwhile, I'll call Stuckup Gallery," Stan told her. "They must not miss out on this opportunity. I looked at your website and your intern did a terrific job. It's not the same as being in the studio, confronting the paintings in person, but I think they'll like your work. I bought a color-field painting from them last year, so perhaps they would take my recommendation seriously. Anyway, we can always try. No accounting for their taste. They might not agree with me. That would be their bad-luck."

"No guarantees with galleries. I'm so used to rejection now, it wouldn't make any difference if they said 'not for us' or simply didn't reply."

"I'll call them tomorrow and ask them to take a serious look at your website."

"Thank you Stan. It always helps to have a recommendation, especially from an important collector!"

"We'll see. It would be great for you to have another show in New York. How long has it been?"

"I'm ashamed to tell you. I don't even know myself. Well, maybe thirty years for a solo show. I've been in group shows there on and off. But no gallery after David Fine ever clicked."

"We'll try him too. He's got that new gallery now. The snow-scenes he showed after he moved to Fifty-Seventh Street and dropped all his contemporary artists didn't cut the mustard!"

"He told me he likes to work with estates. That's a polite way of saying he likes showing dead artists. They don't give him any flak." Joy laughed. "He also told me he didn't want to work with me again because I was a 'tough-cookie.'"

"Gallery owners change their mind," Stan noted. "You have mellowed in your older-age!"

"Yes, I'm not the young rebel I used to be. I've changed from a tough-cookie to a soaked sponge!"

Carey smiled at her friend. So far, she hadn't said a word, just looked in wonder at the paintings. Now she spoke. "I love 'Flame Pond' too. Stan made the best choice. Any gallery that turns you down has to be idiotic."

"Thanks Carey. I don't know how I got into this rejection thing. I never had a problem getting a gallery. I even turned them down. Now, time-after-time, I get the same answer—'not for us.' It's discouraging." Joy shifted her weight from foot-to-foot. She felt weighted down by all the rejection she had experienced in the last few years.

"It's hard to find anything new that's as good as your painting." Stan paced in front of her canvases. "If they show modern masters like Picasso or Gorky, sure, they have a wonderful presentation. But this so-called 'Conceptual Art' is often so boring. I walk into a gallery, yawn, turn around, and walk out."

"Duchamp pulled it off. It was all down-hill after him." Joy observed. "But he created a trend without trying. Nothing has been the same since."

Carey smiled. "Thank God you kept painting! We're going to love living with *Flame Pond*. If Stan's movie is a hit, we are going to live in Beverly Hills!"

"How exciting! I'll go to see it! When will it come out?"

"No telling. You're invited to the premier, however, whenever that takes place," Stan smiled.

"Can't wait! It's going to be terrific. You'll have a big hit on your hands, I'm certain."

"Your words in God's ear," Carey said. "It took two years to write."

"Everything that's worthwhile takes a lot of time. Look at this endeavor of mine. I've been painting forty years."

"It shows!"

"Well, we have a party to attend. The producer invited us." Carey said smiling.

"Have a wonderful time."

"We'll talk next week," Stan reassured. "In the meantime, I'll call Stuckup Gallery. Your show will be the best one they ever had!" Stan gestured his long arms one last time, as if mimicking the paintings.

"I don't know about that. But thank you so much." Joy was smiling broadly as she opened the gate for them to exit. It was so great to have friends who would venture to help her.

And the promised check would get her months of painting time. Her relief was palpable as she cleaned up and prepared to go home to feed Brandy.

Chapter Thirty-Three

Joy brushed a deep blood- red across her canvas. Cadmium red dark was almost gruesome in its depth of color. She would counter it with olive green. The phone rang just as she was envisioning the green she would mix up from the dark red, pthalo blue and golden yellow. It would be almost a muddy olive, giving even more depth to the red.

She put her brush down and ran to answer the ringing.

"Hello Joy. This is Don. I was wondering if that invitation to visit your studio was still open? I finished my show for Miami and the trucking company took the results away this morning."

"Sure. Congratulations on finishing your show! When would you like to come over?"

"How about tomorrow for lunch? You got any good places to eat near you?"

"We have a Thai restaurant within walking distance. The food is good and they have a patio seating surrounded by plants."

"Sounds fine. How about 12:30?"

"Terrific! See you tomorrow."

Joy went back to mixing her olive green. Perhaps the lonely life she feared would not transpire. Perhaps it was all about making new friends and reigniting the old ones.

The next day Don arrived on time. "You've been working!" he noted, as he strode around the studio, his large work boots making a clumping sound. He licked his lips. "These paintings are delicious. You should send some slides to Miami. They still love painting there."

"We built a new website. I had an intern from the Rhode Island School of Design. She helped me construct it. The curators can look at that."

"I thought about Thai food," Don said. "But what I really hanker for today is Mexican. Do you have any good Mexican places around here? I bet you do!"

"Yes, there are two good ones down the street. But we would have to drive as they're too far to walk."

"Can we take your truck? I still haven't gotten around to cleaning out the car."

"I don't see why not. The truck is right here, at your service."

Joy put her brushes into the thinner, turned on her answering machine, and locked the back door.

"I see you have a package to mail," Don said. "Is the post-office on the way?"

"Yes, it is actually." Joy shuddered slightly at the thought of going there. She would have to get over this knee-jerk reaction. There was nothing wrong with the post-office itself. And Don was going to be with her in case she needed protection, a witness, etc. She picked up the package, then let Don out of the gate, following him. She pushed the heavy garage door down with a thud after giving the package to Don to hold.

It was a box of clothes for her mother. Joy had bought a gray sweat-suit of soft cotton and a bright tobacco red-orange Izod knit top that would be comfortable and cheery. Amy had been transferred from the hospital back to the dreary convalescent home. But then Gary had found a smaller nursing home near where she used to live. This gave the neighbors an easier path to visit her.

After her double-whammy combination stroke and Gout attack, Amy could only babble but not talk. However, it looked like she would make her ninety-first birthday. Whether she would walk into P.F. Chang's, however, remained doubtful. She was still bed-ridden, sleeping much of the time. Gary and Joy had worked hard on eliminating many of the "medications" she had been given. It was shocking to Joy that each successive doctor, except for one, had put her on diuretics, the very drug that had caused all the problems in the first place. She wondered about doctors' addiction to prescribing drugs. A medical student she had encountered told her it was not unusual in geriatrics to give twenty or more drugs to patients.

Don got into the passenger seat, putting the package on his lap. Joy let herself into the driver's seat. She started the engine and then pulled a right in order to go around the block. The post-office was in the other direction, as were the two Mexican restaurants they could choose from. She liked the first one best. They had a wonderful soup with chunks of corn-on-the-cob floating in it. She hadn't been there in a long time but Pedro's Grill was a success and they had remodeled. She tried to ignore the queasy feeling in her stomach by thinking of the delicious soup.

Don noticed Joy's slowing to find a spot. "Why don't you go into the parking lot? It's easier and you don't have to pay a meter."

"I avoid the post-office lot like the plague! Remember I told you about the 'accident-stager' who hit me?"

"That was a long time ago. You can't be paranoid the rest of your life!"

"O.K. Yes, you have a point. I've got to conquer my fears." She reluctantly pulled into the lot. Amy would get her comfortable new outfit soon. That was what counted. She was silly to be so fearful. Hadn't Detective Miller told her that Gaude Velasquez would probably never bother her again? That she would probably never even encounter him, as she had made too much trouble for Velasquez, reporting the accident-stager to the police, two detectives, the DMV, and the Child Protection Agency? She laughed at her list.

"What's so funny?" Don asked.

"I gave that accident-stager such a hard time. You're right. He probably figured it's best to avoid me at all costs!" Joy chuckled, as she pulled into the parking lot. Still, she felt weird and her hands shook. Gathering her courage, (she needed courage to mail a package?), she wondered at her fears. She couldn't shake off the ominous atmosphere that suddenly surrounded her. A feeling of panic shot through her. *Joy's instincts told her she should not have parked in the lot, that it was still dangerous.* Joy straightened her posture so she could stop trembling.

Once she had accomplished her task, Joy got back into her truck where Don was patiently waiting. She started the engine, backed up, and headed for the driveway. Looking both ways was mandatory. But, she reminded herself, it hadn't helped before. It had been totally clear both ways when she had pulled out, that fateful day. Velasquez must have been parked, watching the driveway like a hawk for his perfect victim. She shuddered involuntarily, a shot of terror racing through her. She was his perfect victim!

It was once more clear both ways when she pulled out. Joy drove straight ahead on Old York towards the restaurant. Suddenly, she saw Velasquez once more driving in the wrong direction in the opposite lane, staring at her. It was him! This deja-vu was not her imagination. His dirty Benz, paralleling her on the narrow two-lane road with no center divider, was at once repellent and fascinating. His stare was the all-too-familiar race-car driver in an intense competition. Was he nuts? Was she delusional? Joy blinked, but there he was. She was not mistaken, nor was this a figment of her imagination. "It's him!" she breathed. "Look, it's the accident-stager!"

"Pull over quick!" Don pointed to an empty parking space. Joy veered over, her truck screeching to a halt as she swerved into it. The brakes squealed indignantly.

They both looked up. The horror of the scene confronting them took place as if in a slow-motion movie. Gaude had finally taken his eyes off them and was staring straight ahead in disbelief at Jose's tow truck. The large truck with the familiar signage was headed in the same lane, bound west towards her studio. The driver of the truck, the man who had given her such a hard time about his smelly exhaust, stared in disbelief as he met up with the dented, mint-green, smoke-spewing Mercedes, headed East in the West-bound lane.

There was a loud, spine-tingling crash as Joy read "We Buy Cars 4 Cash" and saw Gaude's head and neck being pounded against the windshield. The glass had shattered, cutting his neck which dangled, looking broken, the tendons and bone sticking out. Blood gushed onto the steering wheel. His head lay limp, as if pounded by a club. The horn sounded, stuck from his weight being thrust upon it. The Mercedes crumpled, smashed almost in two, looked like half a car.

The tow-truck driver got out, apparently unharmed, looked over at Joy with wide eyes, raised his arms in disbelief and alarm, and got on his cell phone. His big, heavy truck did not look like it had sustained irreparable damage—a dent or two. But the South American appeared shocked, his face white and his hair standing on end like porcupine quills.

Joy began to sob. Her shoulders shook with emotion and the release of built-up fear and tension. Don took her in his arms and held her while she cried and squealed.

"You were right," Don said softly. "He tried again. He made his second attempt. It was a really crazy thing for him to do. He must be insane! But this time, I was here to help."

"Thank God!" was all she could utter.

Sirens screamed in the near-distance. Soon a police car and a fire engine had arrived. Joy and Don watched in stupefied horror as a policeman tried to remove the remains of Gaude Velasquez from the car. This proved too difficult. The policeman got on his cell-phone to get back-up. A special rescue device would be needed. Gaude hadn't moved an inch. He seemed to be dead as a door-nail. His stiffened body was folded upon the steering wheel. His broken neck met the glass, allowing his head to almost pro-trude out the windshield. He was as still as a dead frozen chicken.

The police were soon talking with the tow-truck operator, trying to determine what had happened. "You'd better go over there," Don said. "I'll go with you."

Joy got out of her truck obediently, like a robot. Don fol-lowed her across the street. Traffic was being cordoned off by the fire-fighters with flares and barriers. More police cars arrived. Someone was taking photographs.

"We're pretty sure we know what happened," Joy told the policeman.

"You witnessed the accident?" The officer was a large-boned man with a weary face. He looked kind, however.

"Yes. You see it's a long story. This man is Gaude Velasquez. He's an accident- stager. He hit my truck last July to collect insurance. There wasn't a witness and he had a lawyer, so my insurance company paid him eleven thousand dollars. He had his kids in the back seat. I gave him a really hard time and it took him five months to get his money. He might have decided to try again, or maybe he wanted to kill me."

The policeman's head turned sideways, like a dog trying to understand a command. "You mean, this was *planned?* He might have attempted to kill you?"

"That may have been his plan. He was angry at me for detaining his insurance money and reporting him as an accident-stager. He figured he had convinced me to take the blame. But I wised up."

"Well, he won't try accident-staging anymore," the policeman let out a whistle. "It's backfired and killed him this time. We're waiting for a special truck to remove him from the tangle. We need you come to the police station, Traffic Central, this afternoon to testify. I'll give you directions."

"I know where it is," Joy laughed ruefully. "I've been there before, as you may have guessed."

"How about around three? I'll have my detective meet you."

"O.K. I just wish he had learned his lesson. I didn't want him to have to die!"

"He did it to himself," the policeman observed. " You didn't have a lot to do with it. You must have pulled over in the nick of time."

"Don saw an empty parking space. I wish it hadn't come down to this. In a way he had talent. He was skilled with a very sharp eye and split-second sense of timing. A good shot! And he had a family. He could have learned to use his skills to help others, making money legally. I feel sorry for him. At first I felt so much anger toward him. But I've come to terms with it. I chanted for his happiness."

"That's nice of you, lady. But if your story is true, I wouldn't give a plug nickel for this character."

Joy nodded. "Crime's a waste of human resources. It may pay in the short run. But karma always comes back to you. It's cause and effect."

The policeman nodded. "How true!"

"How about that Mexican soup?" Don reminded Joy as they crossed the street back to her car. She didn't know if she could eat anything solid but perhaps soup would calm her nerves.

"You bet." She smiled at Don, relieved that this last episode in her life was almost over.

Pedro's Grill had been remodeled. The padded booth seats were now violet with bright red piping. The tables were new redwood. The hostess dressed in a purple matt jersey sheath showed them to a back corner table. She handed them each a dark red menu.

"We know what we want," Joy smiled at Don who nodded. "Please bring the soup with the corn cobs floating in it." For a minute Joy shook off the trauma she felt.

The steaming bowls were soon brought to their table.

The soup *was* comforting. Joy tasted it with a relief that had no comparison with any other meal she had ever experienced.

"Did you ever show with David Fine?" she asked Don.

"Yes. I did one show for him," he recalled. "He sold one work and sent the rest back."

"He sold a lot of work for me. Only a few pieces ever came back. I'm thinking of submitting to him. He saw my website and actually called me."

"If he can sell your work, I don't see why not."

"Would you come to New York?"

"You bet. Someone has got to protect you!"

"You did a terrific job today. Velasquez was out to get me. I have had this ominous feeling for five months that he was after me. I got strange hang-up calls. I get hang-up calls from my friend Stan Moshan too, but he always leaves funny caller I.D. "messages" on my home phone. At the studio, if I get a silent call, I don't know whether to laugh or be afraid!" Joy rolled up a corn tortilla and took a bite. It tasted wholesome and soothing. "I was terrified of the 'accident-stager.' Once Velasquez followed me to the Hollywood Bowl where I was picking up concert tickets."

"You didn't go through that dark tunnel, did you?"

"Yes, I did. I think he may have followed me with a knife."

"Oh my God, Joy. We can't lose you to a lunatic!"

"I'm just so glad you were there today." Quick-thinking on your part saved me!"

"Only too glad to help out."

Joy shuddered. She would never forget Gaude Velasquez. "At last I'm free of him."

She didn't know if it was relief or sadness that suddenly enveloped her.

Chapter Thirty-Four

The Malibu sea glistened with sparkles seemingly thrown toward the bridal party. The glitterati echoed the glistening, as comedians and stars arrived to celebrate Stan's marriage. Their designer color-saturated gowns in rustling taffeta and diaphanous silk chiffons, dark suits and tuxedos added a posh aura to the beach scene.

On an improvised wooden stand, a quartet played Pachelbel's "Cannon in D Minor." Carey glowed in the layered white tulip wedding dress Joy had helped her select during that fated Garment District sojourn. She radiated inner beauty and happiness.

Stan looked very fine in a dark navy-blue Armani suit and bare feet. He kissed Carey full on the lips after saying "I do." Cheers erupted as the actor audience screamed in pleasure. It was a warm day, not hot, and bliss seemed to float in the atmosphere like the sun beaming down on the wedding. The preacher, who wore a Hawaiian shirt and khaki shorts, smiled broadly as he proclaimed Stan and Carey "Man and Wife." Overhead a blimp leisurely sailed the blue sky with "L.A. Wed" printed boldly on its side.

Everyone took off their shoes as the quartet broke into Buddy Holly's "That'll Be the Day" and began to dance. The sand flew as partners were whirled around. Don put his arm around Joy and she was soon caught up in the abandon of movement, flying sand, and laughter. After that dance, Elvis Presley's "It's Now or Never" rang out, causing Don to hold Joy close in a slow dance. An appropriate song for the very long relationship Carey and Stan had enjoyed before Stan finally committed.

Several tunes later, Joy was exhausted but happy. The party was led to the pier where a formal sit-down dinner had been set up. Joy was ecstatic to find herself at the bridal section seated next to Don directly across from Carey and Stan.

"Taking your vows against the backdrop of the infinity and depth of the sea was such a great idea," Joy remarked. "The water seemed to surge with the beating of your hearts."

"Thank you for that comment," Carey smiled. We felt at one with the earth and with each other." The sun of her smile seemed to radiate toward the sun-kissed water. Flickers of light caught her face. Her serene expression put everyone at ease. She exuded bliss.

"I have good news also," Joy smiled at Don and then at the radiant new married couple.

"What's that? You got a show?" Carey asked.

"Yes. How did you guess?"

"With the level of your work, it's no surprise," remarked Stan. "So who is the lucky gallery owner?"

"Bestor Gallery. Tom Bestor is a young Australian. He got some good reviews for an artist of my generation he showed. I saw his review in *Art Ltd* magazine and gave the gallery a call to set up an appointment. My pitch was that if he showed my work during 'Pacific Standard Time' to go with the Getty's program and book, he would get publicity for his gallery. As you know, the Getty is including artists who originated the Los Angeles art world in shows across California in sixty institutions. My work wasn't in any of them, but I thought a gallery might be able to tag along."

"That's a great idea." Don remarked. "He must have liked the idea, and the work, of course."

"His assistant went nuts when she saw my paintings and wanted them immediately, but he said his clients want dark work 'like Francis Bacon.'"

"Really, he didn't take to your joyful paintings?" Carey questioned.

"No. And I just wrote it off as still another rejection."

"So what changed his mind?" Don wanted to know.

"I don't know. He told me the Getty had just named his gallery one of the official 'Pacific Standard Time' galleries, so maybe he thought of me. He e-mailed and asked for my resume. Then I heard nothing for another week. He then e-mailed me an offer for a show in February-March of next year. I accepted. That's the last slot for 'Pacific Standard Time' which starts this October and goes until the end of March."

"Congratulations! We knew you could do it! Maybe he met up with one of your collectors? One who doesn't want only dark paintings?"

"Could be."

"Well, the rejection spell is broken. Where's his gallery?"

"He has two, one on La Brea and one in Santa Monica by the sea on Ocean Boulevard."

"Why don't you propose a two-gallery show? You have plenty of work!" Stan observed. "You have enough works for nine galleries!"

"That's a great idea. I'll do that!"

"Did Stuckup Gallery ever contact you?" Stan asked.

"Yes. Mr. Stuckup said my work was not right for his gallery."

"Well, there are a lot of other galleries in New York. Hundreds! Too bad Stuckup didn't pick up!" Stan laughed again. "How about David Fine?"

"David said he's 'up to his neck' in artists."

"Well, he's strangled in mediocre ones then," Stan commented. "Too bad for him. Did you try anyone else?"

"Oh yes. Several more."

"You'll find the right one. Your show in L. A. will help."

"Thanks. It may rocket me back up or bury me in the sand, depending on what the reaction is. I think it's hard to see new work. My paintings don't look like Francis Bacon, Picasso, or anyone else for that matter. People confront them and feel confused at first. Good new Art should throw you off-balance. It should look like nothing you've seen before. My collector Roman said 'I don't get it, but I'm going to keep looking.'"

"Any new work takes time." Don noted. "The Impressionists were laughed at. People were used to solid colors, not dots of flickering paint and light. They didn't get it."

"Yes. Can you believe the public snubbed their nose at Claude Monet's spectacular 'Water Lilly' mural-sized paintings at first?"

"Is that true?! They must have been bat-blind!" Stan laughed.

"How's your mother doing?" Carey asked.

"She's struggling. She has been in and out of the hospital. Every time she went in, they gave her another CAT-scan! I was furious. The first one was normal. A CAT- scan is equivalent in radiation to three hundred chest X-rays! They gave her three! Gary talked to Dr. Brenner asking why. She said she doesn't look at patients' histories!"

"That's absurd! So where is she now?"

"Gary found a small, private nursing home near her residence. It's a house and admits only eight patients. She has her own bed-room. It's easy to get her on the phone, though after a stroke she can't speak well. We were hoping to get her back to Astrid House, but they don't take bedridden people. Amy is sleeping much of the time. She's alert only for short periods. But she's alive! We're all going up to Reno tomorrow for her ninety-first birthday."

"That's a milestone!" Carey noted. "Keep us informed as to how it goes. We're honeymooning in Tahiti next week. Then getting back to work. The premier is in September! We just found out."

"I can attend?"

"Of course. We want you to be in the 'reserved for special guests' section!"

"Can I bring Don?" She smiled at her companion.

"Yes, we'd also like to see his paintings." Carey looked at Don for his approval.

"I suppose they will have some online from the show." Joy looked at Don.

'Yes, everything is online now!" Don acknowledged.

"Even this wedding?"

"Sure will be." Carey nodded. "There's the video camera with a volunteer cinematographer right over there." She pointed to a small man wielding a large movie camera pointed at their table.

Joy laughed. She drank in the scene: the smiling couple, the long table with their celebrity guests, the sun sinking in the pale blue sky causing it to blush purplish-red. It would make a thrilling video. Carey looked the most beautiful and the happiest that Joy had ever seen her. Stan was enthralled with her. His gaze almost never left her face.

She was so happy for Carey. Stan was the perfect guy for her. And this marvelous ceremony was by far the best she had ever attended. All's well that ends well. She thought of all the great news, parties, premiers and openings that now would fill her schedule. She sighed and smiled at Don who took her hand with a sheepish look on his face.

"Here's to your new life," Joy offered, raising her glass. Everyone mirrored her gesture and a toast was made to the glamorous couple. One by one the comedians made a toast with their comments, suggestions and opinions.

Tina Fey got up and in her best Sarah Palin imitation said, "A toast to Stan and Carey. I came here to attend their wedding and also to harpoon a shark!" Howels of laughter erupted.

Woody Allen then stood up. He was a short, nervous bundle of wire. "I drink to the newlyweds. My advice is: if problems, exigencies and conflicts come up, there is always a way to resolve them. But if worse comes to worse, remember that divorce is preferable to murder."

More nodding and laughter.

Tom Hanks then got up, a tall contrast to Woody Allen. "Here's a toast to Stan and Carey," he said raising his glass. "My advice to the newlyweds is to keep the mystery in the relationship. It's not hard to do this. Simply bring with you to bed a novel by Agatha Christie!" More laughter erupted.

Steve Carell got up next. "I raise my glass to Stan and Carey, two of the most beautiful people on earth! I just finished filming,

Crazy, Stupid Love," he boasted. " My advice is to act crazy and stupid, but be sane and intelligent at the same time! I dare you to try that!"

Everyone nodded and laughed.

Bette Midler then got up in her short skirt, looking like a teenager with boundless energy and her infectious smile. "A toast to the newlyweds!" she said tapping her glass with a knife. "My advice is to take your vows seriously. Be loyal and trustworthy. If you can't be loyal, then at least learn to lie with a straight face!"

Loud guffaws followed this comment.

Will Ferrell then rose up with a tiny, minature basketball he bounced on the table as if he was warming up for a game. "I toast the newlyweds and warn them. Marriage has a tendency to put couples through the hoops!"

More nodding and laughter filled the air.

Betty White stood up. "To the newly married couple. May you live as long and happy a life as I have, without the regrets I've managed to forget about today!"

Everyone nodded in agreement while laughing.

Robin Williams then rose from the table, glass in hand and began his soliloquy. "Marriage is a partnership that provides comfort, security, hugs, and last, but not least, sex. How can you beat that? It provides all the comforts of home, a place to hang your hat, and someone to love you. No one could argue that these benefits are not worthwhile. I love marriage! Getting married is the greatest milestone in life! My advice is that everyone should do it as often possible!"

The party was laughing now so frequently it was hard to think of any problems, whatsoever.

Billy Crystal then got up looking dapper in his tuxedo. He cleared his throat. "The institution of marriage provides everything one needs for a happy life. Someone is there to love, support and encourage you everyday. Life is hard enough; without a partner, it can be miserably lonely. And if you're going to be locked up in an institution, marriage is by far better than the alternatives."

Everyone was howling in unison now.

Rita Rudner raised herself and her glass in unison. "I toast the new bride and groom. As a former ballet dancer and now a comedienne, I no longer tip-toe around the marriage bed. I laugh all through the act!"

"Right on!" someone yelled. Everyone squealed with laughter.

Finally Joy got up "To my wonderful friends! May they live a long and happy life together and collect as much art as possible!"

Everyone nodded in agreement, still laughing until their sides ached.

The sun was sinking, leaving the sky a deep blue with a purplish-red halo. Candles at each setting were being lit by the servers. A quiet hush came over the party. It was the end of the day, and what a day it had been! Everyone was drunk with laughter and champagne.

It had been a day of celebration and toasts, dancing and jubilation.

Joy would be going up to Reno for another celebration the next day: her mother's ninety-first birthday party! Amy would get to meet baby Audrey for the first time, her six-month old great-granddaughter! Joy would spend the whole week in Reno with Amy. The year had passed quickly. So much had happened to her! She had scarcely noticed it zooming by!

After Reno, she would then go to San Francisco to show dealers her new paintings. She would return to the studio and paint for her show next year in February. She would also send large photos of her paintings to New York galleries. Joy had at last broken her rejection spell. She would attempt to extend this winning streak, keep it going, add to it, elaborate on it.

Soon there would be a movie premiere! She would follow up with invitations to all the stars she had just met to see her show of paintings. What a mailing list she would have!

It was time to forget about rejections, accident stagers, and all the traumas she had been through. It was time to feel positive and go forward with her life.

Life should be full of laughter. Life should be fun! Wonderful, memorable times should fill the days. The banquet of life should always be a celebration.

"Let us celebrate every day of our lives!" Joy said to the gathering in general and to Stan and Carey in particular.

THE END

About The Author

AUTHOR and ARTIST Susan Moss has traveled the globe with her two best-selling books, *KEEP YOUR BREASTS!* and *SURVIVE CANCER!* Thousands of lives have been saved from her experience of healing herself of breast and uterine cancer twenty-one years ago, without medical treatment. Her willingness to share her information with others has brought her rich rewards of gratitude from people seeking knowledge on how to prevent and heal cancer naturally.

Moss is also an artist who has shown her work throughout the world. Her paintings, drawings, panels, and new metal-relief drawings have attracted five-hundred collectors including three permanent museum collections: Los Angeles County Museum of Art, Skirball Center, and the Laguna Art Museum. Her first New York gallery show was at David Findlay Jr. gallery on Madison Avenue when she was thirty-two. She also showed thirty oil-crayon drawings at Albright-Knox Gallery in Buffalo, New York. Recently she completed a three gallery show at Bleicher Galleries, Los Angeles and Santa Monica, California.

Her websites are: www.susanhmoss.com and www.susanmoss-art.com

THE ACCIDENT STAGER is her first novel.